P9-CEN-809

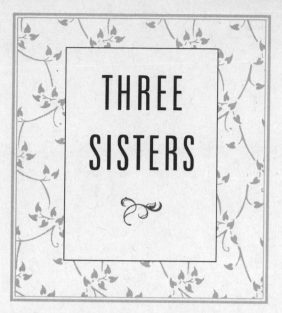

THREE
SISTERS

Textbooks

- A full refund will be given in your original form of payment if textbooks are returned during the first week of classes with original receipt.
- With proof of a schedule change and original receipt, a full refund will be given in your original form of payment during the first 30 days of classes.
- No refunds on unwrapped loose-leaf books or shrink-wrapped titles which do not have the wrapping intact.
- No refunds on Digital Content once accessed.
- Textbooks must be in original condition.
- No refunds or exchanges without original receipt.

General reading books, NOOK® devices, software, audio, video and small electronics

- A full refund will be given in your original form of payment if merchandise is returned within 14 days of purchase with original receipt in original packaging.
- Opened software, audio books, DVDs, CDs, music, and small electronics may not be returned. They can be exchanged for the same item if defective.
- Merchandise must be in original condition.
- No refunds or exchanges without original receipt.

All other merchandise

- A full refund will be given in your original form of payment with original receipt.
- Without a receipt, a store credit will be issued at the current selling price.
- Cash back on merchandise credits or gift cards will not exceed $1.
- No refunds on gift cards, prepaid cards, phone cards, newspapers, or magazines.
- Merchandise must be in original condition.

Fair pricing policy

Barnes & Noble College Booksellers comply with local weights and measures requirements. If the price on your receipt is above the advertised or posted price, please alert a bookseller and we will gladly refund the difference.

NOOK® is a registered trademark of barnesandnoble.com llc or its affiliates.

REFUND POLICY

Textbooks

- A full refund will be given in your original form of payment if textbooks are returned during the first week of classes with original receipt.
- With proof of a schedule change and original receipt, a full refund will be given in your original form of payment during the first 30 days of classes.

ALSO BY LAURENCE SENELICK

The Seagull (translator)

The Cherry Orchard (translator)

The Complete Plays: Anton Chekhov (translator and editor)

Russian Dramatic Theory from Pushkin to the Symbolists

The Chekhov Theatre: A Century of the Plays in Performance

Russian Satiric Comedy (translator)

Gordon Craig's Moscow Hamlet

Serf Actor: The Life and Art of Mikhail Shchepkin

National Theatre in Northern and Eastern Europe (editor)

Historical Dictionary of Russian Theater

THREE
SISTERS

ANTON CHEKHOV

Translated by

LAURENCE SENELICK

W. W. NORTON & COMPANY

NEW YORK   LONDON

Copyright © 2010, 2006 by Laurence Senelick

All rights reserved
Printed in the United States of America
First Edition

For information about permission to reproduce
selections from this book, write to Permissions,
W. W. Norton & Company, Inc.,
500 Fifth Avenue, New York, NY 10110

For information about special discounts for bulk
purchases, please contact W. W. Norton Special Sales
at specialsales@wwnorton.com or 800-233-4830

Manufacturing by Courier Westford
Book design by JAM Design
Production manager: Devon Zahn

Library of Congress Cataloging-in-Publication Data

Chekhov, Anton Pavlovich, 1860–1904.
[Tri sestry. English]
Three sisters / Anton Chekhov ; translated by
Laurence Senelick. — 1st ed.
p. cm.
Includes bibliographical references.
ISBN 978-0-393-33814-0 (pbk.)
I. Senelick, Laurence. II. Title.
PG3456.T8S46 2010
891.72'3—dc22

2010018096

W. W. Norton & Company, Inc.
500 Fifth Avenue, New York, N.Y. 10110
www.wwnorton.com

W. W. Norton & Company Ltd.
Castle House, 75/76 Wells Street, London W1T 3QT

1 2 3 4 5 6 7 8 9 0

This edition is dedicated to the cast and
crew of the Bates College production
directed by Martin Andrucki.

CONTENTS

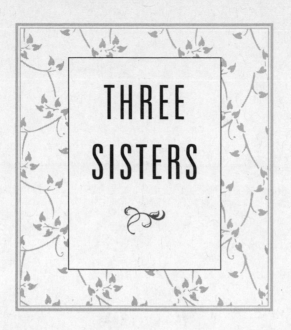

THREE
SISTERS

ANTON CHEKHOV'S BRIEF LIFE

Anton Pavlovich Chekhov was born in the town of Taganrog on the sea of Azov in southern Russia on January 17, 1860,[1] the third of six children, five boys and a girl. He might have been born a serf, as his father, Pavel Yegorovich, had, for the Emancipation came only in 1861; but his grandfather, a capable and energetic estate manager named Yegor Chekh, had prospered so well that in 1841 he had purchased his freedom along with his family's. Anton's mother, Yevgeniya Morozova, was the orphaned daughter of a cloth merchant and a subservient spouse to her despotic husband. To their children, she imparted a sensibility he lacked: Chekhov would later say, somewhat unfairly, that they inherited their talent from their father and their soul from their mother.[2]

The talent was displayed in church. Beyond running a small grocery store where his sons served long hours—"In my childhood, there was no childhood," Anton was later to report[3]—Pavel Chekhov had a taste for the outward trappings of religion. This was satisfied by unfailing observance of the rites of the Eastern

Orthodox Church, daily family worship, and, especially, liturgical music. He enrolled his sons in a choir that he founded and conducted, and he aspired to be a pillar of the community.

Taganrog, its once-prosperous port now silted up and neglected, had a population that exceeded fifty thousand during Chekhov's boyhood. Its residents included wealthy Greek families, the ship-building interests, and a large number of Jews, Tatars, and Armenians. The town benefited from such public amenities of the tsarist civil administration as a pretentious-looking *gymnasium*, which the Chekhov boys attended, for one of Pavel's aims was to procure his children the level of education needed for entry into the professions. The upward mobility of the Chekhov generations is reflected in the character of Lopakhin in *The Cherry Orchard*, a self-made millionaire whose ancestors had been serfs on the estate he succeeds in purchasing. Chekhov's father, born a serf, had risen from *meshchanin*, or petty bourgeois,[4] to be the member of a merchant guild; and Chekhov himself, as a physician and writer, became influential on the national scene. He was a model of the *raznochinets*, or person of no settled rank, who began to dominate Russian society in the latter half of the nineteenth century.

To impede mass advancement, the tsarist curriculum laid great stress on Greek and Latin. One recalls the schoolmaster Kulygin in *Three Sisters* chuckling over the fate of a classmate who missed promotion because he could not master the *ut consecutivum* construction. Schoolmasters are usually portrayed by Chekhov as narrow-minded, obsequious, and unimaginative, no doubt the result of his own observations as he studied the classics,

German, Russian, and, for a brief time, French. His best subject was Scripture. School days were lightened by the fairy tales of his nanny, the picaresque reminiscences of his mother, vacations spent on the estate his grandfather managed, fishing, swimming, and, later, visits to the theater.

As a boy, Chekhov was stage-struck. Although it was against school regulations, he and his classmates, often in false whiskers and dark glasses, frequented the gallery of the active and imposing Taganrog Playhouse. He was also the star performer in domestic theatricals, playing comic roles such as the Mayor in *The Inspector* and the scrivener Chuprun in the Ukrainian folk opera *The Military Magician*. While still at school, he wrote a drama called *Without Patrimony* and a vaudeville (a farce with songs) called *The Hen Has Good Reason to Cluck*. Later, while a medical student, he tried to revise them, even as he completed another farce, *The Cleanshaven Secretary with the Pistol*, which his younger brother Mikhail recalls as being very funny. Never submitted to the government censorship office, which passed plays or forbade them from performance, it is now lost.

By 1876 Pavel Chekhov had so mismanaged his business that, fearing imprisonment for debt, he stole off to the next town, where he took the train to Moscow. There his two elder sons, Aleksandr and Nikolay, were pursuing their studies. He had already stopped paying his dues to the merchant guild and had reverted to the status of *meshchanin*. Whether Anton suffered a psychic trauma at this loss of caste, as had the young Henrik Ibsen when *his* father went bankrupt, is matter for speculation. Certainly, the repercussions felt at the sale of the home left their trace on many of his plays, including *Platonov* and *The Cherry Orchard*. Dispossessed of home and furniture, his mother and the three youngest children also departed for Moscow, abandoning Anton in a house now owned by a friend of his father's. He had to support himself by tutoring during the three years before he graduated. He did not rejoin his family until Easter 1877, his fare paid by his university-student brother Aleksandr. This first visit to Moscow and its theaters set standards by which he henceforth judged the quality of life in the provinces. Suddenly, Taganrog began to look provincial.

Just before Anton Chekhov left Taganrog for good, a public library opened. This enabled him to read classics such as *Don Quixote* and *Hamlet*, a work he was to cite recurrently, and, like any Victorian schoolboy, *Uncle Tom's Cabin* and the adventure stories of Thomas Mayne Reid. Heavier reading included philosophic works that enjoyed a high reputation at the time, such as Thomas Henry Buckle's positivist and skeptical survey of European culture, *The History of Civilization in England*. Later in life, Chekhov took a wry view of this omnivorous autodidacticism, and had the clumsy bookkeeper Yepikhodov in *The Cherry Orchard* allude to Buckle's works as a token of self-improvement.

It was at this time that Chekhov began writing prose, sending comic pieces to Aleksandr in Moscow in the hope that they would be accepted by the numerous comic journals that had sprung up in the capitals. He made friends with actors, hung around backstage, and learned how to make up his face. Two of his school fellows did enter the profession: Aleksandr Vishnevsky, who would become a charter member of the Moscow Art Theatre, and Nikolay Solovtsov, who was to create the title role in *The Bear*.

In 1879 Chekhov moved to Moscow to enter the medical school at the university, funded by a scholarship from the Taganrog municipal authorities. He arrived to find himself the head of the family, which was still in dire straits and living in a cramped basement flat in a disreputable slum. His father, now a humble clerk in a suburban warehouse, boarded at his office; Aleksandr, a journalist, and Nikolay, a painter, led alcoholic and bohemian lives; his three younger siblings, Ivan, Mariya, and Mikhail, still had to complete their educations. Lodging at home, Chekhov was compelled to carve out a career as a journalist at the same time that he was taking the rigorous five-year course in medicine.

At first, he wrote primarily for humor magazines, contributing anecdotes and extended jokes, sometimes as captions to drawings by Nikolay and others; these brought in a niggardly ten to twelve kopeks a line. Gradually, he diversified into parodies, short stories, and serials, including a murder mystery, *The Shooting Party*, and a romance that proved so popular it was filmed several times in the days of silent cinema (*Futile Victory*). He was a reporter at the trial of the CEOs of a failed bank. He became a close friend of Nikolay Leykin, editor of the periodical *Splinters of Petersburg Life*, to which he was a regular contributor from 1883. He conducted a theatrical gossip column, which won him entry to all the greenrooms and side-scenes in Moscow. And he partook of his brothers' bohemianism. He wrote to an old school chum in a letter his Soviet editors provided only in expurgated form: "I was on a spree all last night and, 'cept for a 3-ruble drunk didn't . . . or catch . . . I'm just about to go on a spree again."[5] His writing at this time was published under a variety of pseudonyms, the best known being Antosha Chekhonte, from a schoolboy nickname. He also found time to revise *Without Patrimony*, which he seriously hoped would be staged; turned down by the leading actress to whom he submitted it, it was burnt by its author. Chekhov always took failure in the theater hard. However, two variant copies survived, minus the title page. It was first published in 1923. It has since become known as *Platonov*, after the central character.

The year 1884 was critical in Chekhov's life. At the age of twenty-four, he set up as a general practitioner and, influenced by reading the English social critic Herbert Spencer, began research on a history of medicine in Russia. That December he had bouts of spitting blood, which his medical expertise might have led him to diagnose as a symptom of pulmonary tuberculosis. No outside observer would have suspected this active, well-built, handsome young man was suffering from a mortal illness. Only in his last years did he become a semi-invalid, and, until that time, he kept up the pretence that his symptoms were not fatal. This subterfuge was not carried on simply to allay his family's anxieties. He wilfully strove to ignore the forecast of his own mortality and regularly discounted the gravity of his condition.

Eighteen eighty-four also saw the publication of his first collection of stories, pointedly entitled *Fairy Tales of Melpomene*: the muse of tragedy compressed into pithy anecdotes of the life of actors. Chekhov had found more prestigious and better-paying periodicals to take his stories and was now an expert on Moscow life.

He had an opportunity to amplify his subject matter when he and his family began to spend summers in the country, first with his brother Ivan, master of a village school, and then in a cottage on the estate of the Kiselyov family. It was during those summers that Chekhov gained first-hand knowledge of the manor house setting he employed in many of his plays, and made the acquaintance of the officers of a battery, who turn up as characters in *Three Sisters*. Chekhov's artistic horizons also expanded, for the Kiselyovs, intimates of the composer Chaikovsky, were devoted to classical music. Another summer visitor to become a lifelong friend was the painter Isaak Levitan, whose impressionistic landscapes are graphic counterparts of Chekhov's descriptions.

The following year Chekhov's literary career took a conspicuous upward turn. On a visit to St. Petersburg, Chekhov had been embarrassed by the acclaim that greeted him, because he recognized that much of his output had been hasty and unrevised. "If I had known that that was how they were reading me," he wrote his brother Aleksandr, on January 4, 1886, "I would not have written like a hack." Such stories as "Grief" and "The Huntsman," both from 1885, had already displayed a new care in technique and seriousness in subject matter. Shortly thereafter, he received a letter from Dmitry Grigorovich, the *doyen* of Russian critics, singling him out as the most promising writer of his time and urging him to take his talent more seriously. Although Antosha Chekhonte continued to appear in print for a few more years, Anton Chekhov made his first bow in the powerful Petersburg newspaper *New Times*. Its editor, Aleksey Suvorin, had risen from peasant origins to become a tycoon and a leading influence-monger in the conservative political camp. He and Chekhov were to be closely allied, although their friendship would later founder when Suvorin promoted the anti-Semitic line during the Dreyfus affair.

During the years when he was winning recognition as a writer of short stories, Chekhov made two further attempts to write for the theater. With the first, *Along the Highway* (1885), he came up against the obstacle of the censor, who banned it on the grounds that it was a "gloomy, squalid play." The other piece, the monologue *The Evils of Tobacco*, was, like many of his early "dramatic études," written with a specific actor in mind. It first appeared in 1886 in a St. Petersburg newspaper, and Chekhov kept revising it, publishing the final version, virtually a new work, in his collected writings of 1903. Farces he sketched out with collaborators never got beyond the planning stage.

Between 1886 and 1887, Chekhov published one hundred and sixty-six titles while practicing medicine. Such fecundity boosted his fame but wore him out. His health and his temper both began to fray. Profiting from an advance from Suvorin, Chekhov returned to southern Russia in 1887, a trip that produced remarkable work. The stories that ensued signaled his emergence as a leading writer of serious fiction. The novella "The Steppe" (1888) was published in *The Northern Herald*, one of the so-called fat, or weighty, journals that had introduced the writing of Ivan Turgenev and Lev Tolstoy and served as organs of public opinion. That same year, Chekhov was awarded the Pushkin Prize for Literature by the Imperial Academy of Science for his collection *In the Gloaming*. One of the most enthusiastic instigators of this honor had been the writer Vladimir Nemirovich-Danchenko, who would later play an important role in establishing Chekhov's reputation as a dramatist.

The Northern Herald was liberal in its politics, its editor, Aleksey Pleshcheev, a former prisoner in Siberia with Dostoevsky. Typically, Chekhov was able to be friendly with Pleshcheev and Suvorin at the same time, and he continued to contribute to *New Times*. His reluctance to be identified with any one faction exposed him to much acrimonious criticism from members of both camps, and especially from the progressive left. The writer Katherine Mansfield pointed out that the "problem" in literature is an invention of the nineteenth century. One of the legacies of Russian "civic criticism" of the 1840s was the notion that a writer had an obligation to engage with social problems and offer solutions, making his works an uplifting instrument of enlightenment. This usually meant espousing a doctrinaire political platform. Chekhov, perhaps fortified by his medical training, treasured his objectivity and steadfastly refrained from taking sides, even when his sympathies were easy to ascertain. "God keep us from generalizations," he wrote. "There are a great many opinions in this world and a good half of them are professed by people who have never had any problems."

Between 1886 and 1890, his letters discuss his objectivity and his "monthly change" of opinions, which readers preferred to see as the views of his leading characters. To his brother Aleksandr he insisted on May 10, 1886, that in writing no undue emphasis be placed on political, social, or economic questions. In another letter to Suvorin, on October 27, 1888, Chekhov wrote that the author must be an observer, posing questions but not supplying the answers. It is the reader who brings subjectivity to bear. Not that an author should be aloof, but his own involvement in a problem should be invisible to the reader, he explained to Suvorin, on April 1, 1890:

> You reproach me for my objectivity, calling it indifference to good and evil, absence of ideals and ideas, etc. You want me to say, when I depict horse thieves: horse-stealing is a bad thing. But that's been known for a long time now, without my help, hasn't it? Let juries pass verdicts on horse thieves; as for me, my work is only to show them as they are.

The year before "The Steppe" appeared, Chekhov had at last had a play produced; the manager Fyodor Korsh had commissioned *Ivanov* and staged it at his Moscow theater on November 19, 1887. It was a decided if controversial success. As Chekhov wrote to Aleksandr, "Theater buffs say they've never seen so much ferment, so much unanimous applause *cum* hissing, and never ever heard so many arguments as they saw and heard at my play" (November 20, 1887). It was taken up by the Alexandra Theatre, the Imperial dramatic playhouse in St. Petersburg, and produced there on January 31, 1889, after much hectic rewriting in an attempt to make the playwright's intentions clearer and to take into account the strengths and weaknesses of the new cast.

The theme of a protagonist fettered by a sick wife and want

of money was a distorted reflection of Chekhov's own situation. His family obligations kept his nose to the grindstone, and he felt guilty whenever he traveled away. Yet the success of *Ivanov* and the curtain-raisers *The Bear* and *The Proposal* (1888–1889) had put Chekhov at a premium as a dramatist. Urged on by Korsh and others, and unable to make headway on a full-length novel, Chekhov hoped to collaborate with Suvorin on a new comedy; when the publisher begged off, Chekhov completed it himself as *The Wood Goblin* (1889). It was promptly turned down by the state-subsidized theaters of Petersburg and Moscow, which regarded it as more a dramatized story than an actable play. They recommended that Chekhov give up writing for the stage. A production at a private theater in Moscow was received with apathy bordering on contempt, and may have helped provide the impetus for a decision Chekhov would soon make to go to Sakhalin, ten thousand miles away. Throughout 1888 and 1889, Chekhov also tended to his brother Nikolay, who was dying of tuberculosis; after Nikolay's death, Chekhov experienced both guilt and a foreboding of his own mortality, which brought on the mood conveyed in "A Dismal Story" (1889), in which a professor of medicine contemplates his frustrated ideals and imminent demise. The author's mood was at its lowest ebb.

Secure in his reputation and income at the age of thirty, Chekhov sought to cast off this despondency by traveling to Sakhalin, the Russian Devil's Island, in 1890; the eighty-one-day journey was arduous, for the Trans-Siberian railway had not yet been built. The enterprise may have been inspired by a Tolstoyan wish to practice altruism or it may have been an ambitious project to write a magnum opus of "medical geography." In any case, the ensuing documentary study of the penal colony was a model of socially engaged field research, and may have led to prison reforms. On a more personal level, it intensified a new strain of pessimism in Chekhov's work, for, despite his disclaimers, he began to be bothered by his lack of outlook or mission.

No sooner had Chekhov returned, via Hong Kong, Singapore, and Ceylon, than he made his first excursion to Western Europe, accompanying Suvorin. His initial enthusiasm for Vienna, Venice, and Naples began to wane by the time he visited Nice, Monte Carlo, and Paris, and he was eager to get back to work. In Russia, with the writing routines resumed, the sense of enslavement returned. This mood was modulated by a flirtation with a family friend, Lidiya (Lika) Mizinova, who invested more significance in the relationship than he did. Her subsequent affair and illegitimate child with the married writer Ignaty Potapenko would be exploited by Chekhov in *The Seagull* (although he hoped his own circle would not spot the similarities).

The steady flow of royalties enabled Chekhov in 1891 to buy a farmstead at Melikhovo, some fifty miles south of Moscow, where he settled his parents and siblings. There he set about "to squeeze the last drop of slave out of his system" (as he wrote to Suvorin on January 7, 1889); "a modern Cincinnatus," he planted a cherry orchard, installed a flush toilet, and became a lavish host. This rustication had a beneficial effect on both his literary work and his humanitarianism. He threw himself into schemes for building roads and schools and opened a clinic to provide free medical treatment, improving peasants' minds and bodies. During the cholera epidemic of 1892–1893, he served as an overworked member of the sanitary commission and head of the famine relief board. These experiences found their way into the activities of Dr. Astrov in *Uncle Vanya*.

During this period, Chekhov composed masterful stories that explored the dead ends of life: "The Duel" (1891), "Ward No. 6" (1892), "The Black Monk," "A Woman's Kingdom," "The Student" (all 1894), "Three Years" (1895), "The House with the Mansard," "My Life" (both 1896), and "Peasants" (1897), carefully wrought prose pieces of great psychological subtlety. They recurrently dwell on the illusions indispensable to making life bearable, the often frustrated attempts at contact with one's fellow man, the inexorable pull of inertia preventing people from realizing their potential for honesty and happiness. Chekhov's attitude is clinically critical, but always with a keen eye for the sympathetic details that lead the reader to a deeper understanding.

For several years, Chekhov abandoned the theater, except for some monologues and one-act farces. Not until January 1894 did he announce that he had again begun a play, only to deny it a year later, in a letter to V. V. Bilibin: "I am not writing a play and, altogether, I have no inclination to write any. I am grown old, and I have lost my burning ardor. I should like to write a novel 100 miles long" (January 18, 1895). Nine months after that he was to break the news to Suvorin, "Can you imagine, I am writing a play which I shall probably not finish before the end of November. I am writing it not without pleasure, though I swear horribly at the conventions of the stage. A comedy, three women's parts, six men's, four acts, a landscape (view of a lake); a great deal of conversation about literature, little action, five tons of love" (October 21, 1895).

The comedy was *The Seagull*, which had a rocky opening night at St. Petersburg's Alexandra Theatre in 1896: the actors misunderstood it, the audience misapprehended it. Despite protestations of unconcern to Suvorin ("I dosed myself with castor oil, took a cold bath—and now I would not even mind writing another play"; October 22, 1896), Chekhov fled to Melikhovo, where he renounced playwriting. Although *The Seagull* grew in public favor in subsequent performances, Chekhov disliked submitting his work to the judgment of literary cliques and claques. Yet barely one year after the event, a new drama from his hand appeared in the 1897 collection of his plays: *Uncle Vanya*, a reworking of the earlier *The Wood Goblin*. It was widely performed in provincial capitals, where the residents found it reflected their dreary lives.

It was during this year that Chekhov's illness was definitively diagnosed as tuberculosis, and he was compelled to leave Melikhovo for a milder climate. For the rest of his life, he shuttled between Yalta on the Black Sea and various French and German spas, with occasional business trips to Moscow. He had a house constructed in the Yalta suburb of Autka. To pay for it, and to cover the new expenses his multiple residences created, Chekhov sold all he had written before 1899, excepting the plays, to the publisher Marks for the flat fee of 75,000 rubles (in current purchasing power, approximately $81,000), along with the reprint rights to any future stories. It was an improvident move. Marks had had no idea of the size of Chekhov's output and had underpaid. The error in calculation may have induced Chekhov to return to playwriting as a more lucrative activity.

The remainder of his dramatic career was bound up with the fortunes of the Moscow Art Theatre, founded in 1897 by his friend Nemirovich-Danchenko and the wealthy dilettante K. S. Alekseev, who acted under the name Konstantin Stanislavsky. Chekhov was one of the original shareholders in the enterprise. He admired his friends' announced program of ensemble playing, their serious attitude to art, and a repertory of high literary quality. At the opening production, Aleksey Tolstoy's blank-verse historical drama *Tsar Feodor Ioannovich*, his eye was caught by Olga Knipper, the young actress who played the tsarina. With only slight misgivings Chekhov allowed the Art Theatre to revive *The Seagull* at the close of its first season. Stanislavsky, as co-director, had greater misgivings; he did not understand the play. But a heavily atmospheric production won over the audience, and the play was a resounding success. The Moscow Art Theatre adopted an art-nouveau seagull as its insignia and henceforth regarded Chekhov as its house dramatist. When the Imperial Maly Theatre insisted on revisions to *Uncle Vanya*, which had been playing throughout the provinces for years, Chekhov withdrew the play from them and allowed the Art Theatre to stage its Moscow premiere. *Three Sisters* (1901) was written with Art Theatre actors in mind.

Chekhov's chronic reaction to the production of his plays was revulsion, and so two months after the opening of *Three Sisters*, he was declaring, to Olga Knipper, "I will never write for the theater again. One can write for the theater in Germany, in Sweden, even in Spain, but not in Russia, where dramatists get no respect, are kicked by hooves and forgiven neither success nor failure" (March 1, 1901). Nevertheless, he soon was deep into *The Cherry Orchard* (1904), tailoring the roles to specific Moscow Art players. Each of these productions won Chekhov greater fame as a playwright, even when he himself disagreed with the chosen interpretation of the Art Theatre.

Chekhov languished in Yalta, which he called his "warm Siberia," feeling that he had been shunted to an outpost for the moribund. At the age of forty, in 1900, to the great surprise of his friends and the temporary dismay of his sister Mariya, who had always been his housekeeper, he married the Art Theatre actress Olga Knipper. Chekhov's liaisons with women had been numerous, ranging from a brief engagement in 1886 to Dunya Efros, a Jewish woman who refused to convert to Orthodoxy, to a one-night stand with a Japanese prostitute and a fling with the flamboyant actress Lidiya Yavorskaya. He exercised an involuntary fascination over a certain type of ambitious bluestocking and his fan mail from female admirers was considerable. Some women friends, such as Lidiya Avilova, projected their desires onto an ordinary relationship, casting themselves as Chekhov's Egeria. Whenever the affair became too demanding or the woman too clinging, Chekhov would use irony and playful humor to disengage himself. In his writings, marriage is usually portrayed as a snare and a delusion that mires his characters in spirit-sapping vulgarity. His relationship with Knipper was both high-spirited—she was his "kitten," his "horsie," his "lambkin," his "darling crocodile"—and conveniently remote, for she had to spend much of her time in Moscow, while he convalesced at his villa in Yalta. On those terms, the marriage was a success.

Chekhov's villa, today a museum, became a Mecca for young writers, importunate fans, touring acting companies, and plain freeloaders. Such pilgrimages, though well meant, were not conducive to Chekhov's peace of mind or body, and his health continued to deteriorate. Despite this rapid decline, and the disappointment of a miscarriage Olga suffered in 1902,[6] a deeply lyrical tone suffuses his last writings. His late stories, "The Darling" and "Lady with Lapdog" (both 1899) and "The Bishop" (1902) and "Betrothed" (1903), offer more acceptance of the cyclical nature of life. They also reveal an almost musical attention to the structure and sounds of words, a quality to be remarked as well in the last "comedy," *The Cherry Orchard*.

In December 1903, a failing Chekhov came to Moscow to attend rehearsals of *The Cherry Orchard*. The opening night, January 17, 1904, concided with his name day and the twenty-fifth anniversary of the commencement of his literary activity. Emaciated, hunched over, gravely ill, he did not show up until the second act and sat through the third, after which, to his great bemusement, a ceremony to honor him took place.

In June 1904 the Berlin doctors Chekhov consulted ordered him to Badenweiler, a health resort in the Black Forest. There the forty-four-year-old writer died on July 2. Shortly before his death, the doctor recommended putting an ice pack on his heart. "You don't put ice on an empty heart," Chekhov protested. When they suggested a glass of champagne, his last words came, "It's been a long time since I've drunk champagne." Unconsciously, he echoed the line of the old nurse Marina in *Uncle Vanya*: "It's a long time since I've had noodles."

Chekhov's obsequies were a comedy of errors he might have appreciated. The railway carriage bearing his body to St. Petersburg was stencilled with the label "Fresh Oysters," and, at the Novodevichy cemetery in Moscow, the bystanders spent more time ogling the controversial author Maksim Gorky and the bass singer Fyodor Shalyapin than in mourning the deceased.[7] Finally, and inadvertently, Chekhov's cortège became entangled with that of General Keller, a military hero who had been shipped home from the Far East. Chekhov's friends were startled to hear an army band accompanying the remains of a man who had always been chary of the grand gesture.

NOTES

1 The date given by Chekhov himself, although he would appear to have been born on the 16th. The 17th was his "saint's day" or "name day," the day of St. Anthony after whom he was christened. Dates given here are "Old Style," in accord with the Julian calendar, twelve days behind the Gregorian.

2 M. P. Chekhov, *Vokrug Chekhova* (Moscow: Moskovsky rabochy, 1980), p. 44.

3 Quoted in Ernest Simmons, *Chekhov, A Biography* (Boston: Little, Brown, 1962), p. 6.

4 Peter the Great had established a table of ranks that stratified social status into civil, military, naval, and ecclesiastical hierarchies. In the civil hierarchy, *meshchanin* (literally, townsman) came just above peasant. In *The Seagull*, Treplyov complains that his father had been classified as a *meshchanin* of Kiev, even though he was a famous actor, and the same rank appears on his own passport. He finds it particularly galling since the term had come to imply philistinism.

5 Letter to Dmitry Savelyov, January (?) 1884. All translated quotations from Chekhov's writings and letters are based on *Polnoe sobranie sochineny i pisem*, the

complete collected works and letters in thirty volumes published in Moscow in 1974–1983. On the cuts made by Soviet editors, see A. Chudakov, " 'Neprilichnye slova' i oblik klassika. O kupyurakh v izdaniya pisem Chekhova," *Literaturnoe obozrenie* (November 1991): 54–56.

6 Olga's miscarriage is described in a letter of hers to Chekhov (March 31, 1902). However, a controversy has arisen among scholars as to whether it was a miscarriage, an ectopic pregnancy, or something else; moreover, the paternity of the child has been questioned. See the articles of Hugh McLean and Donald Rayfield in *The Bulletin of the North American Chekhov Society* XI, 1 (Summer 2003), and letters in subsequent issues.

7 Maksim Gorky, *Literary Portraits*, trans. Ivy Litvinov (Moscow: Foreign Languages Publishing House, n.d.), pp. 158–159.

CHRONOLOGY OF CHEKHOV'S LIFE

1860. *January 17* (Old Style) / *29* (New Style). Anton Pavlovich Chekhov, third son of the shopkeeper and choirmaster Pavel Yegorovich Chekhov and Yevgeniya Yakovlevna Morozova, is born in Taganrog, a port of the Sea of Azov. He is the grandson of a serf who managed to purchase his liberation.

Aleksandr Ostrovsky's play *Thunderstorm* wins an award from the Academy of Sciences.

1861. Tsar Alexander II abolishes serfdom, but without providing enough land for the emancipated serfs.

1862. Ivan Turgenev's *Fathers and Sons* is published.

Academic freedom restored to Russian universities.

1863. Flogging with birch rods abolished by law.

Konstantin Stanislavsky is born, as Konstantin Alekseev, son of a wealthy textile manufacturer.

Nikolay Chernyshevsky's *What Is to Be Done?*, the gospel of nihilism, is written in prison.

1864. *Zemstvos*, self-governing rural councils, are created.

1865. Lev Tolstoy begins to publish *War and Peace*.

1866. An attempted assassination of the tsar prompts a wave of political reaction, especially in education and the press. Chekhov, as a student, will suffer from the new emphasis on Greek, Latin, and grammar.

Fyodor Dostoevsky's *Crime and Punishment* published.

1867–1879. Chekhov's primary and secondary education in Taganrog in very rigorous schools. He gives lessons, frequents the theater, edits a student newspaper, writes plays now lost.

1868. Dostoevsky's *The Idiot* is published serially.

1871. Dostoevsky's *The Devils* is published.

1872. Special court set up to try treason cases.

1873. Only 227 factories in all of Russia.

Nikolay Nekrasov begins to publish his populist poem *Who Can Be Happy in Russia?*

1874. Trade unions made illegal.

All males over twenty-one, regardless of class, now liable for conscription into the armed forces.

1875. Chekhov writes comic journal *The Stutterer* to amuse his brothers in Moscow.

Tolstoy begins to publish *Anna Karenina*.

1876. Chekhov's father goes bankrupt and moves the family to Moscow, leaving Anton in Taganrog.

1877. Chekhov visits Moscow where he finds his family in penury.

The Russians fight the Turks in the Balkans, ostensibly to free the Christian Slavs from Moslem oppression. An armistice, signed in 1878, greatly reduces the Turkish presence in the Balkans, but the Congress of Berlin humiliates Russia by reducing its spoils to part of Bessarabia.

1878. Chekhov writes plays now lost: *Without Patrimony, He Met His Match*, and *The Hen Has Good Reason to Cluck*.

Public outcries against the government and acts of terrorism increase.

1879. Chekhov finishes high school and in June moves to Moscow, where he enrolls in the medical school of the University of Moscow on a scholarship. Starts to write cartoon captions for the humor magazine *Alarm Clock*.

Dostoevsky begins to publish *The Brothers Karamazov*.

1880. *March.* Chekhov's first short story, "Letter of a Landowner to His Learned Neighbor Dr. Friedrich," is published in the comic journal *The Dragon-fly*.

1880–1887. Chekhov writes for Moscow and St. Petersburg comic journals under pen names including Antosha Chekhonte, Doctor Who's Lost His Patients, Man without a Spleen, and My Brother's Brother.

1881. Chekhov writes play later known as *Platonov* (not published until 1923).

Tsar Alexander II is assassinated; his son, Alexander III, initiates a reign of political repression and social stagnation.

Dostoevsky dies.

1882. *Platonov* is turned down by the Maly Theatre. Chekhov publishes "Late-blooming Flowers."

The imperial monopoly on theater in Moscow and St. Petersburg is abolished. Several private theaters are opened.

Troops are used to suppress student uprisings at the Universities of St. Petersburg and Kazan.

1883. Chekhov publishes "Fat and Lean," "At Sea," and "Christmas Eve."

1884. Chekhov finishes his medical studies and starts general practice in Chikino, outside Moscow. Publishes his first collection of stories, *Fairy Tales of Melpomene*, under the name Antosha Chekhonte. His only attempt at a novel, *The Shooting Party*, serialized in *Daily News*. Writes one-act play, *Along the High Road*, which is censored and not published until 1914.

December. Symptoms of Chekhov's tuberculosis diagnosed.

1885. Chekhov's first trip to St. Petersburg. Meets the publisher Aleksey Suvorin and the painter Isaak Levitan, who become close friends. Romances with Dunya Efros and Nataliya Golden. Publishes "The Huntsman," "Sergeant Prishibeev," and "Grief."

1886. Chekhov begins writing for Suvorin's conservative newspaper *New Times*. Puts out a second collection of stories, *Motley Tales*, signed both An. P. Chekhov and Antosha Chekhonte.

The eminent Russian critic Dmitry Grigorovich encourages him to pursue his literary career in a more serious fashion. Publishes "The Witch," "The Chorus Girl," "On the Road," and the first version of the comic monologue *The Evils of Tobacco*.

1887. Chekhov publishes third collection of short stories, *In the Gloaming*, and fourth collection, *Innocent Conversations*, which include "Enemies," "Typhus," "The Siren," and "Kashtanka." Also writes one-act *Swan Song*.

November 19. Ivanov, a full-length play, performed at Korsh's Theatre, Moscow. It receives a mixed press.

1888. First serious long story, "The Steppe," published in St. Petersburg magazine *Northern Herald*, initiating a new care taken with his writing. One-act farces *The Bear* and *The Proposal* produced to acclaim. *In the Gloaming* wins the Pushkin Prize of the Academy of Sciences.

Student uprisings at the Universities of Moscow, Odessa, Kharkov, and Kazan are put down by the military. The government decrees that all Jews must live within the Pale of Settlement in Eastern Poland and the western provinces of Russia.

Tolstoy publishes his play of peasant life *The Power of Darkness*, but the censor will not allow it to be staged.

Maksim Gorky is arrested for subversion, and is henceforth under police surveillance.

1889. The Social Democratic Working-man's Party is founded.

"A Dismal Story," one of the first of Chekhov's mature stories, published in *Northern Herald*.

January 31. Premiere of the revised *Ivanov* at Alexandra Theatre, St. Petersburg.

October. Chekhov's play *The Wood Goblin* finished. Played at Abramova's Theatre in *December*. The play is poorly received by the critics; he is scolded for "blindly copying everyday life and paying no attention to the requirements of the stage."

1890. According to a letter to Sergey Dyagilev, Chekhov reworks *The Wood Goblin* into *Uncle Vanya*, which will not be published until 1897. Chekhov publishes collection *Glum People*, which includes "Thieves" and "Gusev." Writes one-act comedies, *The Involuntary Tragedian* and *The Wedding*.

April–October. Travels through Siberia to Sakhalin Island, where he visits prison camps and carries out a census. Sails in the Pacific and Indian Oceans.

1891. Six-week trip to Western Europe. Publication of the novella *The Duel* and "Peasant Women." Buys a small farmstead in Melikhovo.

1892. Chekhov settles in Melikhovo with his family.

Work begins on the Trans-Siberian Railway, to be completed in 1905.

Sergey Witte becomes Minister of Finance, and turns Russia into a modern industrial state, increasing industrialism, railways, and Western trade by 1899.

1892–1893.   Severe famines in the grain-growing provinces in the south and along the Volga.

Chekhov acts as head of the district sanitary commission during the cholera epidemic, combats the famine, treats the poorest peasants for free.

Publishes eleven stories, including "My Wife," "The Grasshopper," "Ward No. 6," as well as the one-act farce *The Celebration*.

1893.   Dalliance with Lika Mizinova, whom he decides not to marry, but who sees herself as a prototype for Nina in *The Seagull*. *The Island of Sakhalin* published serially. Publishes "An Anonymous Story" and "Big Volodya and Little Volodya."

1894.   Second trip to Italy and to Paris. Health worsens. Publishes "The Student," "Rothschild's Fiddle," "The Head Gardener's Story," "The Literature Teacher," "The Black Monk," and "At a Country House."

Alexander III dies and is succeeded by his son, the conservative and vacillating Nicholas II.

1895.   *The Island of Sakhalin* published. Chekhov meets Lev Tolstoy at his estate Yasnaya Polyana.

Chekhov writes *The Seagull*, publishes "Three Years," "Ariadne," "His Wife," "Whitebrow," "Murder," and "Anna Round the Neck."

1896.   Chekhov sponsors the construction of a primary school in the village of Talezh. Serial publication of "My Life" and "The House with a Mansard."

October 17. The premiere of *The Seagull* at the Alexandra

Theatre in St. Petersburg fails. Chekhov flees during the second act.

October 21. Relative success of the play at its second performance.

1896–1897. Strikes of factory workers lead to a law limiting adult work to eleven and a half hours a day.

1897. The first All-Russian Congress of Stage Workers meets in Moscow to argue questions of trade conditions and artistic principles.

Stanislavsky and Nemirovich-Danchenko found the Moscow Art Theatre.

Chekhov sponsors the construction of a primary school in the village of Novosyolky. Participates in the All-Russian census of the population. Father dies.

March–April. Hospitalized with first acute attack of pulmonary tuberculosis. Reads Maurice Maeterlinck.

September. Travels to France for medical treatment.

Uncle Vanya, Ivanov, The Seagull, and one-act plays published, as well as stories "Peasants," "The Savage," "At Home," and "In the Cart."

1898. Thirteen thousand students at Moscow University go on strike to protest repressive moves on the part of the administration; orders are given to enlist them in the army.

May. Chekhov returns from abroad. Relations with Suvorin strained in connection with the Dreyfus trial.

September. Settles in Yalta after suffering a pulmonary hemorrhage. Publishes the stories "Calling on Friends," "Gooseberries," "About Love," "A Case History," and "Ionych."

December 17. *The Seagull*, staged by Stanislavsky, is revived with great success at the Moscow Art Theatre.

1899. Theatres in Kiev, Kharkov, and Nizhny Novgorod play *Uncle Vanya*. Chekhov decides to turn it into a short novel, but does not. Offered to the Maly, *Uncle Vanya* is considered offensive to professors and is turned down.

Tolstoy's *Resurrection* and Gorky's *Foma Gordeev* published.

Chekhov attends a performance of *The Seagull* in Yalta. Sells all rights to his works to the publisher A. F. Marks for 75,000 rubles (in current purchasing power, approximately $81,000). Begins to edit his complete works. Awarded Order of St. Stanislas, second class, for work in education. Publishes "On Official Business," "Lady with Lapdog," "The Darling," and "The New Villa."

June. Sells his estate in Melikhovo. Has a house built in Yalta.

October 26. Premiere of *Uncle Vanya* at the Art Theatre.

1900. *January.* Elected to honorary membership in the Literary division of the Academy of Sciences. Publishes "In the Ravine" and "At Christmas."

April. The Art Theatre plays *Uncle Vanya* and *The Seagull* in Sevastopol, in the presence of the author.

August–December. Writes *Three Sisters.* Finishes the play in Nice.

1901. *January–February.* Trip to Italy.

January 31. Premiere of *Three Sisters* at the Moscow Art Theatre with considerable success.

May 25. Marries the actress Olga Knipper, who plays Masha.

The Marxist journal *Life*, which publishes Gorky, is banned.
Gorky is expelled from Nizhny Novgorod.

1902. Chekhov publishes "The Bishop." Complete works pub-
lished in eleven volumes. Awarded Griboedov Prize of Society of
Dramatic Authors and Opera Composers for *Three Sisters.* Begins
The Cherry Orchard.

March. Olga Knipper suffers miscarriage.

August. Resigns in protest from the Academy of Sciences when
Gorky's election is nullified at the tsar's behest.

Gorky writes *The Lower Depths.*

1903. At a Congress in London, the Social Democratic
Working-man's Party is taken over by the radical Bolshevist wing,
led by Vladimir Lenin.

Second edition of Chekhov's complete works published in six-
teen volumes.

Publishes his last story, "Betrothed," in the magazine
Everybody's.

June. The censor rules that his plays cannot be performed in
people's theaters, low-priced theater for the working class.

September. The Cherry Orchard is finished. Nemirovich-
Danchenko and Stanislavsky are enthusiastic. Chekhov attends
rehearsals.

An atrocious pogrom occurs in Kishinyov, with 47 dead and
2,000 families ruined.

1904. Chekhov's health deteriorates.

January 14 or 15. Attends a rehearsal of *The Cherry Orchard.*

January 17. Premiere at the Art Theatre, where a celebration in his honor is held.

Spring. A new, grave attack of tuberculosis.

April 2. First performance of *Orchard* in St. Petersburg a great success, greater than in Moscow, according to Nemirovich and Stanislavsky.

June 1. Publication of the play in a separate edition by Marks.

June 3. Departure for Germany with Olga Knipper.

July 2/15. Dies in Badenweiler.

July 9/22. Buried in Novo-devichy cemetery in Moscow.

The Mensheviks drive the Bolsheviks from the Central Committee of the Social Democratic Working-man's Party, but drop out the following year, leaving the field to the Bolsheviks.

The Russo-Japanese war breaks out.

1909. First performance of a Chekhov play in English: *The Seagull,* translated by George Calderon, at the Glasgow Repertory Theatre.

A NOTE ON THE TRANSLATION

The text on which this translation is based is that in A. P. Chekhov, *Polnoe sobranie sochineniy i pisem v tridtsati tomakh* (*Complete Works and Letters in Thirty Volumes*), edited by N. F. Belchikov et al. (Moscow: Nauka, 1974–1984). The Russian text was drawn from the latest version published in Chekhov's lifetime and subject to his revision.

Chekhov had his doubts about the efficacy of translation, and after reading some Russian prose translated into French, concluded that transmission of Russian literature into another language was pointless. Later, when his own plays began to be translated, he lamented that purely Russian phenomena would have no meaning for foreign audiences. To offset these misgivings, the translator of Chekhov must be as sedulous in making choices as the author was in composing the original work.

From his earliest farces, Chekhov wrote plays with an eye to their being performed. He often had specific actors in mind, and, despite his discomfort with histrionic convention, he expected his dialogue to be recited from the stage. Therefore, translating his plays entails problems different from those encountered in translating his prose fiction. At first sight, the vocabulary and sentence structure seem straightforward enough. Under scrutiny, however, the seeming simplicity turns out to be illusory.

The literary psychoanalyst Gregory Zilboorg, initiating American readers into Russian drama in 1920, stated point-blank that Chekhov was fundamentally untranslatable, more so even than Aleksandr Ostrovsky and Maksim Gorky. "Chekhov's plays lose their chief element in translation into whatever other language: the particular harmony and rhythm of the original. The student must bear in mind that studying Chekhov's drama in English he actually studies only some elements of them, the rest being lost in a foreign language."[1]

The "harmony and rhythm" so lost derive from a number of sources. First, Chekhov uses language to consolidate his major plays: recurrent phrases echo off one another, often for ironic effect. George Bernard Shaw was another playwright well aware that it was precisely this adhesive repetition of key words that knit a play together. He scolded his German translator,

> The way in which you translate every word just as it comes and then forget it and translate it some other way when it begins (or should begin) to make the audience laugh, is enough to whiten the hair on an author's head. Have you ever read Shakespear's Much Ado About Nothing? In it a man calls a constable an ass, and throughout the rest of the play the constable can think of nothing but this insult and keeps on saying, "But forget not, mas-

ters, that I am an ass." Now if you translated Much Ado, you would make the man call the constable a Schaffkopf. On the next page he would be a Narr, then a Maul, then a Thier, and perhaps the very last time an Esel.[2]

This was such a salient principle for Shaw that he hammered at it the following month: "I tell you again and again most earnestly and seriously, that unless you repeat the words that I have repeated, you will throw away all the best stage effects and make the play unpopular with the actors . . . Half the art of dialogue consists in the echoing of words—the tossing back & forwards of phrases from one to another like a cricket ball . . ."[3]

What is true for Shaw is equally true for Chekhov. A commonplace uttered in the first act may return to resonate with fresh significance. In *Three Sisters*, the phrases *vsyo ravno* (it doesn't matter, it's all the same) and *nadoelo* (fed up, sick and tired) recur regularly, sometimes with ironic effect, depending on who is speaking. The words for "hard work" and "labor" recur regularly. It is the translator's obligation to preserve these verbal *leitmotifs* as much as possible.

Lexical and etymological elements subliminally affect the atmosphere. Literary allusions to the Russian classics (Pushkin, Lermontov, Gogol, Krylov, Ostrovsky) illustrate the cultural context. For the educated Russian of Chekhov's time, they would have been immediately familiar. In the milieu of *Three Sisters*, populated by educators and well-read military men, bandying quotations is a common pastime. Although Kulygin's Latin tags are clearly a sign of his pedantry, the household words mouthed by the other characters represent the rags and tatters of culture to which they cling, a *patois* meant to distinguish them from the likes of Natasha.

In his last plays, Chekhov is extremely careful in choosing his words. Every character speaks in a particular cadence. Although both Vershinin and Tusenbach spout speeches about the future, one can tell merely by the tone and phrasing which one is speaking. Their speech patterns are so characteristic that others can imitate them. There is also a class difference in the way the intelligentsia and the servants express themselves.

Harder to pin down is the "specific gravity" of a statement that resides in its structure. Russian can reassemble the elements of a sentence to make a particular emphasis; English has to find a way of reproducing this. Mere phrasebook translation, offering a direct statement, can betray the subtle emphases of the original.

Finally, certain words and phrases that held a special meaning in Chekhov's time may require that an explanation be embedded in the translation, particularly if it is meant to be performed. Who is the unpronounceable Poprishchin referred to? Why does a samovar offered as a birthday gift shock the company? How does one convey the fact that Balzac's marriage in Berdichev is strange, because Berdichev is known to be a predominately Jewish town?

The same applies to jokes. Chekhov often plants *jeux de mots* and facetious phrasing as depth charges; the translator's first task is to be aware of them, the second to find a way of making them detonate properly. Kulygin's ponderous witticism that the Latin word *renixa* resembles the Cyrillic чепуха, "nonsense," may be lame, but the translator has to find an equivalent, all the same.

These peculiarities of Chekhov add to the usual problems experienced in translating from Russian: the passive constructions, the distinction between verbs of imperfect and perfect action, and onomatopoeic sounds that are overlooked or scanted.

"The shock of the new" in Chekhov's handling of dialogue contributed mightily to his reputation in his lifetime, but today this aspect tends to be lost or overlooked. As Nils Åke Nilsson pointed out, Chekhov is an unacknowledged precursor of the Futurists and their launching of a *zaumny*, or transrational language. He cites as examples the phrase "You've Gavril-ed it up enough" in *Ivanov*, the trom-tom-tom exchange in *Three Sisters*, and Gaev's billiard jargon in *The Cherry Orchard*, calling this a "new dramatic syntax."[4]

The American critic Stark Young, when he set out to translate *The Seagull* for the Lunts in 1938, singled out "those balances, repetitions for stage effect, repetitions for stage economy, theatrical combinations and devices, time-patterns, and so on, that are the fruits of much intention and technical craft, and that are almost totally absent from the translation.[5] Yet even he trembled before Chekhov's linguistic audacity: "Chekhov's dialogue is perhaps a trifle more colloquial than mine. Certainly it is more colloquial than I should ever dare to be; for in a translation any very marked colloquialism is always apt to hurt the economy of effect by raising questions as to what the original could have been to come out so patly as that."[6]

Consequently, Young was very cautious in rendering the joki-ness of Chekhov's dialogue and sought a simplicity that dena-tures the special flavor of the language. In this respect, Chekhov is very deceptive. His lexical choices and often straightforward syntax enable him to be used in the classroom; but this seeming simplicity overlies a deliberate restriction of vocabulary. Conse-quently, unusual words and phrases stand out all the more. In addition, the sentence structure is organized poetically in order to express character and, as an actor of the time would put it, make points. Translators, led astray by Chekhov's poker-faced approach (in some respects similar to Mark Twain's), have often made him sound more wooden and monotonous, less fruity and lyrical, than he is.

Finally, I have not tried to pretend that Chekhov is anything other than Russian. Although I have converted weights and mea-sures into Western equivalents so that an audience can more eas-ily gauge distances and density, I have left currency, beverages, and, in particular, names in their Russian forms. Modern read-ers and audiences rapidly adjust to patronymics, diminutives, and nicknames. If one is to turn Andrey into Andrew and Masha into Mary, then one must go the whole hog and refer to Solyony as Salteen and, to be consistent, *Uncle Vanya* as *Uncle Jack*.

NOTES

1 Gregory Zilboorg, "A course in Russian drama," *The Drama* (Nov. 1920): 69.

2 *Bernard Shaw's Letters to Siegfried Trebitsch*, ed. Samuel A. Weiss (Stanford:

Stanford University Press, 1986), p. 30 (26 Dec. 1902). The words translate as "sheep's head," "fool," "muzzle," "beast," "ass."

3 Ibid., 15 Jan. 1903, p. 36.

4 Nils Åke Nilsson, "Two Chekhovs: Mayakovskiy on Chekhov's 'futurism,'" in Jean-Pierre Barricelli, ed., *Chekhov's Great Plays: A Critical Anthology* (New York: New York University Press, 1981), pp. 251–61.

5 Stark Young, "Translating *The Sea Gull*," in *The Sea Gull*, A *Drama in Four Acts*, translated from the Russian of Anton Chekhov by Stark Young (New York: Samuel French, 1950), pp. xii–xv.

6 Ibid., p. xix.

PRONUNCIATION GUIDE

Andrey Sergeevich (Sergeich) Prozorov (Andryusha, Andryushan-chik) *ahn-DRAY sir-GAY-yeh-veech (sir-GAY-eech)*
PRAW-zah-raaff (ahn-DRYOO-sha, an-DRYOO-shahn-cheek)

Natalya Ivanovna (Natasha) *nah-TAHL-yah ee-VAHN-ahf-nah (na-TAH-sha)*

Olga Sergeevna (Olyushka, Olya) *AWL-gah sir-GAY-ehf-nah (AWL-yoosh-kah, AWL-yah)*

Masha (Mariya Sergeevna, Mashka, Mashenka) *MAH-sha (mah-REE-yah sir-GAY-ehf-nah, MAHSH-kah, MAH-shehn-kah)*

Irina (Arinushka, Arisha) *ee-REE-nah (ah-REE-noosh-kah, ah-REE-shah)*

Fyodor (Fedya) Ilyich Kulygin *FYAW-dahr (FYEHD-yah) eel-EECH koo-LEE-gheen*

Aleksandr Ignatyevich Vershinin *ah-lick-SAHND'r eeg-NAHT-yeh-veech vir-SHEE-neen*

Nikolay Lvovich Tusenbach *nee-kah-LIE l'VAW-veech TOO-zehn-BA'H*

Vasily Vasilyevich Solyony *vah-SEE-lee vah-SEEL-yeh-veech sahl-YAWN-ee*

Ivan Romanovich (Romanych) Chebutykin *ee-VAHN rah-MAHN-ah-veech (rah-MAHN-eech) cheh-boo-TEE-keen*

Aleksey Petrovich Fedotik *ah-lick-SAY pit-RAW-veech fyeh-DAW-teek*

Vladimir Karlovich Rodé *vlah-DEE-meer KAHR-lah-veech rah-DAY*

[53]

Ferapont *fir-ah-PAWNT*
Anfisa *ahn-FEE-sah*
Basmanny *bahs-MAHN-nee*
Berdichev *bir-DEE-chehf*
Bobik *BAW-beek*
Bolshoy *bahl-SHOY*
Chekhartma *cheh-'hahrt-MAH*
Cheremsha *cheh-rehm-SHAH*
Chita *chee-TAH*
Dobrolyubov *dah-brah-LYOO-bahf*
Kirsanovsky *keer-SAHN-ahf-skee*
Kochane *kah-'HAHN-eh*
Kolotilin *kah-lah-TEE-leen*
Kozyrev *KAW-zee-ryehf*
Krasny *KRAHS-nee*
Lermontov *LYEHR-mahn-taff*
Marfa *MAHR-fah*
Moskovsky *mahs-KAWFF-skee*
Nemetskaya *nyeh-MYEHT-sky-ah*
Novo-Devichy *NAW-vah-DYEH-vee-chee*
Potapych *pah-TAH-peech*
Protopopov, Mikhail Ivanych *prah-tah-PAW-pahff,
mee-'high-EEL ee-VAH-neech*
Pyzhikhov *PEE-zhee-kahff*
Saratov *sah-RAH-tahff*
Skvortsov *skvahr-TSAWF*
Spiridonych *spee-ree-DAWN-eech*
Stanislav *STAHN-ee-slahv*
Testov *TYEHS-tahf*
Tsytsykar *tsee-tsee-KAHR*
Zasyp *zah-SEEP*

INTRODUCTION

At the urging of the Moscow Art Theatre, Chekhov set out to write them a play. With specific actors in mind for given roles, and mindful, too, of the Art Theatre's strengths, Chekhov spent more time in the composition of *Three Sisters* than on any of his earlier dramas. He was especially anxious to cut out superfluities in monologues and provide a sense of movement.

Unfortunately, when the Art Theatre actors heard the author read the play for the first time, in October 1900, they were sorely disappointed. "This is no play, it's only an outline" was the immediate reaction. Chekhov sedulously reworked all of it and in the process added many striking touches. The ironic counterpoint of Tusenbach's and Chebutykin's remarks in Acts One and Four, most of Solyony's pungent lines, Masha's quotation from *Ruslan and Lyudmila* about the curved seashore were added at this stage. It is amazing to think that only in revising the play did Chekhov decide to leave Masha on stage for the final tableau. He sat in on the early rehearsals and insisted that a colonel be in attendance to instruct the actors in proper military deportment; he personally orchestrated the fire-bell sound effects for Act Three. He put the greatest emphasis on that act, which, he insisted, must be performed quietly and wearily.

Three Sisters opened on January 31, 1901, with Stanislavsky as Vershinin, Olga Knipper as Masha, and the young Vsevolod Meyerhold as Tusenbach. Although many critics were put off by the play's seeming hopelessness and what struck them as vague motivation in the characters, the production was acclaimed by the public. "It's music, not acting," asserted Maksim Gorky.[1]

The writer Leonid Andreev attended the thirtieth performance, despite a friend's warning that its effect would be suicidally depressing. Quite against expectation, he found himself totally drawn into the play by the middle of Act One. No longer appraising the scenery or the actors, he became convinced that "the story of the three sisters . . . is not a fiction, not a fantasy, but a fact, an event, something every bit as real as stock options at the Savings Bank." By the end, he, with the rest of the audience, was in tears, but his dominant impression was not pessimistic. For Andreev, the residual effect, the pervasive mood, the play's basic "tragic melody" was a yearning for life. "Like steam, life can be compressed into a narrow little container, but, also like steam, it will endure pressure only to a certain point. And in *Three Sisters*, this pressure is brought to the limit, beyond which it will explode, —and don't you actually hear how life is seething, doesn't its angrily protesting voice reach your ears?"[2]

This reaction was due in part to the play's early run coinciding with student riots. Consequently, the characters' aspirations were identified with topical political protest. It was due as well to the

theater's remarkably veristic production and its careful transmission of mood. Eventually, theatergoers would say not that they
were going to the Art Theatre to view *Three Sisters* but that they
were "paying a call on the Prozorovs." Chekhov's technique provided the premise for this illusion of reality.

This is the first time Chekhov employs a broad canvas devoid of
exclusively foreground figures. The sisters must share their space,
in every sense, with Natasha, Tusenbach, and Solyony. There
are no more soliloquys: almost never is a character left alone on
stage. Andrey must pour out his discontents to deaf Ferapont, and
Masha must proclaim her adulterous love to the stopped-up ears
of her sister Olga. Têtes-à-têtes are of the briefest. Vershinin and
Tusenbach spout their speeches about work and the future to a
room full of auditors.

Those rhetorical paeans have been cited as Utopian alterna-
tives to the dreary provincial life depicted on stage. True, the men
who formulate them are ineffectual, with no chance of realizing
their "thick-coming fantasies." But the monologues do work as
a meliorative element. Unable in a play to use the narrative to
offer a contrasting vision, Chekhov must put into the mouths of
his characters visions of an improved life. The imagery of birds
of passage, birch trees, flowing rivers sounds a note of freshness
and harmony that highlights all the more acutely the characters'
inability to get in touch with the spontaneous and the natural.
The cranes are programmed to fly, "and whatever thoughts, sublime or trivial, drift through their heads, they'll go on flying, not
knowing what for or where to."

The most blatant call for an alternative is the sisters' recur-

rent plaint, "To Moscow, to Moscow!" Almost from the play's premiere, critics wondered what was stopping the Prozorovs from
buying a ticket to the big city. Moscow is an imaginary site, envis-
aged differently by each character. Andrey sees it not only as a
university town but as the site of great restaurants, while for old
Ferapont it marks the locale of a legendary pancake feast. Vershinin gloomily recalls a grim bridge and roaring water there, Solyony has invented a second university for it, and Olga looks back
to a funeral. No clear image emerges from the medley of impressions, so that Moscow remains somewhere over the rainbow, just
out of sight.

Because the sisters are fixated on this distant point, commen-
tators and directors have regularly inflated them into heroines.
Too frequently, the play is reduced to a conflict between three
superwomen and a ravening bitch: The sensitive and high-strung
Prozorov sorority can be no match for the ruthless life force
embodied in Natasha, and so they succumb, albeit preserving
their ideals. This common interpretation is not borne out by a
close examination of the play, which Chekhov said had *four* heroines. As the Romanian critic Jovan Hristić has shrewdly noted,
the three of the title are "true spiritual sisters of Hedda Gabler,
who corrupt everything around them by dint of thinking themselves superior."[3] The analogy works on several levels, from the
military upbringing (Masha's scorn of civilians is bitter) to the
ultimate downfall, engineered partly by an instinctual bourgeoise
(Natasha for Thea Elvsted), second-rate academics (Andrey and
Kulygin for Tesman), and inept idealists (Vershinin and Tusenbach for Løvborg). Like Hedda, the three sisters are at variance

with their environment, which, for them, represents common vulgarity.

The play maps the town's encroachment on their lives, as Olga becomes embedded in the educational hierarchy, Irina turns into a cog in the civil bureaucracy, Andrey a fixture on the County Council, and Masha a recalcitrant faculty wife. By the last act, the stage direction informs us that their backyard has become a kind of empty lot, across which the townsfolk tramp when necessary. It is the next step after the fire, when the townsfolk invaded their home and bore off their old clothes. And, of course, Natasha's depredations and that of her lover and the town's de facto head, the unseen Protopopov, began earliest of all.

To protect themselves against this encroachment, the sisters have erected a paling of culture, and within it, they have invited the military. For once, Chekhov does not use outsiders as a disruptive force; for the sisters, the soldiers spell color, excitement, life. But the factitiousness of this glamour quickly becomes apparent: A peacetime army is a symbol of idleness and pointless expense. Men trained to fight while away their time philosophizing and playing the piano, teaching gymnastics and reading the paper, carrying on backstairs love affairs and fighting duels. The sisters have pinned their hopes on a regiment of straw men. It is hard to determine who is the weakest: Vershinin, forecasting future happiness while unable to cope with his psychotic wife; Tusenbach, whose noble sentiments are belied by his unprepossessing looks and unassertive manner; or Solyony, veering crazily between blustering egotism and crippling introspection. These are carpet knights, suitable for dressing out a party but not for salvaging anyone's life. That the sisters should make such a fuss about them reveals at once the irreality of their values.

If culture, in the sense of refined feelings revealed through sensitivity and a cultivated understanding of art, is the touchstone for the Prozorovs, it will not sustain scrutiny either. The Prozorov family prides itself on the Russian intellectual's virtues of political awareness, social commitment, and artistic discrimination, and judges others by them. Many of the major characters are connected with the educational system. When tested by the realities of life, however, the fabric of their culture soon falls to pieces. They and their circle cling to the shreds and patches—Latin tags for Kulygin, quotations from Russian classics for Masha and Solyony, amateur music-making. Andrey's "sawing away" at the violin and Masha's untested prowess at the keyboard are mocked in the last act by Natasha's offstage rendition of the "Maiden's Prayer." Irina grieves that she cannot remember the Italian for *window*, as if a foreign vocabulary could buoy her up in a sea of despair. Solyony poses as the romantic poet Lermontov, but his behavior shows him to be more like Martynov, the bully who killed Lermontov in a duel. During the fire, it is Natasha who must remind Olga of the cultured person's duty "to help the poor, it's an obligation of the rich." Philosophizing (always a pejorative word for Chekhov) passes for thought, newspaper filler passes for knowledge, a superior attitude passes for delicacy of feeling, yet everyone's conduct sooner or later dissolves into rudeness or immorality.

Three Sisters does not simply demonstrate how three gifted women were defeated by a philistine environment, but rather how their unhappiness is of their own making. If they are subjugated and evicted by the Natashas of this world, it is because they have not recognized and dealt with their own shortcomings. At one point or another, each of the sisters is as callous and purblind as Natasha herself. Olga cattily criticizes Natasha's dress sense at a party, although she has been told that the girl is shy in company; in Act Three she refuses to listen to Masha's avowal of love, will not face facts. Her very removal to a garret is as much avoidance of involvement as it is an exile imposed by Natasha. Irina is remarkably unpleasant to both her suitors, Tusenbach and Solyony; as a telegraph clerk she is brusque with a grieving mother, and at the very last refuses to say the few words of love that might lighten the Baron's final moments, even though, as Chekhov informed Olga Knipper, she is prescient of the impending catastrophe. Masha swears like a trooper, drinks, abuses the old nanny nearly as badly and with less excuse than Natasha does. Her flagrant adultery with Vershinin may ultimately be more destructive than Natasha's with Protopopov, for Kulygin genuinely loves his wife, whereas Andrey tries to forget he has one.

This litany of faults is not meant to blacken the sisters or to exonerate Natasha, Solyony, and the others. It is meant to redress the balance: Chekhov selects the Prozorov family (who, along with the officers, were based on acquaintances) to sum up a way of life. With all the benefits of education, a loving home, and creature comforts, the sisters stagnate, not simply because they live in the sticks but because they keep deferring any activity that might give meaning to their existence. The ennobling labor that Tusenbach and Vershinin rhapsodize over, that inspires Irina, seems to have nothing in common with doing a job every day.

Olga's teaching, Irina's work at the Council and the telegraph office, the position at the mines to which Tusenbach retires offer a prospect of meaningless drudgery.

The prevalent state of mind is to be "sick and tired" (*nadoelo*). In his brief moment alone with Masha in Act Two, Vershinin blames the average local educated Russian for being "sick and tired of his wife, sick and tired of his estate, sick and tired of his horses;" but he is clearly characterizing himself, for he soon draws a picture of his own wretched marriage. Masha, whom Vershinin would exempt as an exceptional person, is "sick and tired of winter," and when her husband proclaims his love with "I'm content, I'm content, I'm content!" she bitterly spits back, "I'm sick and tired, sick and tired, sick and tired." Even the genteel Olga pronounces herself "sick and tired" of the fire. The unanimous response to this spiritual malaise is a commonplace fatalism. Chebutykin's dismissive "It doesn't matter" (*Vsyo ravno*) is echoed by most of the characters. Vershinin quotes it when denying differences between the military and civilians; Tusenbach describes his resignation from the army in those words; Solyony denigrates his love for Irina with the phrase. According to Irina, Andrey's debts "don't matter" to Natasha. This deliberate insouciance is the counterbalance to the equally deliberate velleities about the future.

To represent the slow disintegration of these lives, *Three Sisters* unfolds over a longer period of time than any of Chekhov's other plays. It begins on the fifth of May, Irina's twentieth nameday, and ends in autumn, four years later. The characters talk incessantly about time, from the very first line. The passage of time is denoted by such obvious tokens as Natasha's growing children, Andrey's problem with his weight and his debts, Olga's promotions. However, this is more than a family chronicle. Chekhov insists on the subjectivity of time. Each act indicates that what had gone before is now irrevocably swallowed up, not lost simply in the distant past, but in what had been yesterday. The youth in Moscow, aglow with promise, to which the sisters retrospect is tarnished by their initial response to its witness, Vershinin: "Oh, how you've aged!" The party in Act One is spoken of in Act Two, a few months later, as if it belonged to a bygone Golden Age. By Act Three, Tusenbach is referring to it as "Back in those days." Time measures the increasing negativity of life; it has been two years since the doctor took a drink, three years since Masha played the piano, or maybe four. It's been a long time since Andrey played cards—that is, the few months since Act Two. If time passes in a steady process of diminution, perspectives into the future are not enough to replace the losses. Chebutykin smashes a valuable clock, demolishing time, but his chiming watch in the last act continues to announce fresh departures.

Setting up markers for time, Chekhov constructs each act around a special event that catalyzes routine responses and sticks in the memory. Irina's nameday celebration serves a number of dramatic functions: It commemorates a date, assembles all the characters in one place, and is the highwater mark for the sisters' hopes. It is the last time we see them as sole mistresses in their own domain: Each of them is on the verge of a promising situation. Coming of age opens the world to Irina; the arrival of Vershinin enlivens Masha; and Olga still enjoys teaching. The Shrovetide party in Act Two is in sharp contrast: It takes place after dark, with several habitués absent (Olga and Kulygin must work late, Vershinin is delayed by his wife's suicide attempt). Twice the party is broken up by the usurper Natasha, from whom no masqueraders are forthcoming. Finally, the revelers realize that amusement must now be sought outside this home.

The eating at these events, a metaphor for shared experience, disintegrates as the play proceeds. Act One has ended with the cast gathered around the table, regaling themselves with roast turkey, apple pie, and too much vodka. The odd men out were Natasha and Andrey, furtively conducting their romance at a remove from the teasing family. In Act Two, however, Natasha is now seated at the festive board, criticizing the table manners of others and withholding tea; Solyony has eaten up all the chocolates. Once she gains a foothold, the indiscriminate feeding ends. Vershinin goes hungry.

The fire in Act Three is a real *coup de théâtre*: Physical danger, mass hysteria, and crowd movement, though kept offstage, have forced the characters into their present situation, both locally and emotionally. Like Andreev's image of steam rising in a boiler, they gradually are forced upward into the compressed space beneath the eaves. Even though the conflagration does not singe the Prozorov house, it creates this thermodynamic effect. Exhausted or drunk, in some way pushed to an extreme by the calamity, the characters pour out their feelings and then leave. It is the most hysterical of all the acts and the most confessional. To no avail does Olga protest, "I'm not listening, I'm not listening!" Unlike purifying fires in Ibsen and Strindberg, this blaze leaves the sisters uncleansed, as their world is rapidly being consumed. Amidst the desolation, they are simply charred.

Once again, Chekhov constrains his characters to come in contact by preventing privacy. One would expect the bedroom of an old-maid schoolmarm and a young virgin to be the most sacrosanct of chambers, but a concatenation of circumstances turns it into Grand Central Station, from which intruders like Solyony and Chebutykin must be forcibly ejected. The space is intimate, just right for playing out personal crises, but the secrets are made to detonate in public. The doctor's drunken creed of nihilism, Andrey's exasperation with his wife, Masha's blurting out of her adultery become public events.

Or else the private moment is neutralized by submersion in minutiae. Masha makes up her mind to elope with Vershinin. Traditionally, this would be a major dramatic turning point, the crux when the heroine undergoes her peripeteia. Here, the decision is muffled by plans for a charity recital, Tusenbach's snoring, and other people's personal problems. The chance tryst offered by the fire trivializes Masha's and Vershinin's love because it projects it against a background of civic crisis. Even their love song has been reduced to "trom-tom-tom," humming a theme from an operatic aria. What is crucial to some characters is always irrelevant or unknown to others. As Chebutykin says, "It doesn't matter." Chekhov, however, does not insist on the impossibility of values and communication; he simply believes that the attribution of value is hard for myopic mortals to make.

The last act adjusts the angle of vantage. There is very little recollection in it, but a good deal of futile straining toward the future.

A brief time has elapsed between Act Three, when the regiment's departure is offhandedly mentioned, and Act Four, when it takes place. The departure is so abrupt an end to the sisters' consoling illusion that they cannot bring themselves to allude to the past. Henceforth they will be thrown on their own resources. The play had begun with them lording it over the drawing room, but now they are cast into the yard. Olga lives at the school, Masha refuses to go into the house, Andrey wanders around with the baby carriage like a soul in limbo. Food has lost its ability to comfort. The Baron must go off to his death without his morning coffee, while Andrey equates goose and cabbage with the deadly grip of matrimony. Each movement away is accompanied by music: The regiment leaves to the cheerful strains of a marching band, the piano tinkles to the cozy domesticity of Natasha and Protopopov, and the Doctor mockingly sings "Tarara boom de-ay." The bereft sisters standing in the yard are made to seem out of tune.

The final tableau, with the sisters clinging to one another, intoning "If only we knew, if only we knew," has been played optimistically, as if the dawn of a bright tomorrow did lie just beyond the horizon. But Olga's evocation of time to come has lost the rosy tinge of Vershinin's and Tusenbach's improvisation. It is whistling in the dark and predicts a void that must be filled. The disillusionment of the four hours' traffic on the stage and the four years' passage of time has aged the sisters but not enlightened them. They still, in William Blake's words, "nurse unacted desires." The music-hall chorus Chebutykin sings had lyrics (which would have been known to everyone in the original audience): "I'm sitting on a curbstone / And weeping bitterly / Because I know so little." The implied mockery shows Olga's "If only we knew" to be an absurd wish. Chekhov's antiphony of Olga and Chebutykin carols the impossibility of such awareness, and the need to soldier on, despite that disability.

NOTES

1 Maksim Gorky, *Sobranie sochineniya* (Moscow: Akademiya Nauk SSR, 1958), XXVIII, 159.

2 Leonid Andreev, "Tri sestry," *Polnoe sobranie sochineny* (St. Petersburg: A. F. Marks, 1913), VI, 321–25.

3 Jovan Hristić, *Le théâtre de Tchékhov*, trans. Harita Wybrands and Francis Wybrands (Lausanne: L'Âge d'homme, 1982), p. 166.

THREE SISTERS

Три сестры

A Drama in Four Acts

CAST OF CHARACTERS [1]

PROZOROV, ANDREY SERGEEVICH

NATALIYA IVANOVNA, *his fiancée, afterwards his wife*

OLGA
MASHA — *his sisters*
IRINA

KULYGIN, FYODOR ILYICH, *high school teacher,*
Masha's husband

VERSHININ, ALEKSANDR IGNATYEVICH, *Lieutenant*
Colonel, battery commander

TUSENBACH, NIKOLAY LVOVICH, *Baron, Lieutenant*

---

1 Ironically, Prozorov suggests "insight, perspicuity," and Vershinin "heights, summit." Solyony means "salty." The name of the unseen Protopopov hints at descent from a line of archpriests.

SOLYONY, VASILY VASILYEVICH, *Staff Captain*

CHEBUTYKIN, IVAN ROMANOVICH, *army doctor*

FEDOTIK, ALEKSEY PETROVICH, *Second Lieutenant*

RODÉ,[2] VLADIMIR KARLOVICH, *Second Lieutenant*

FERAPONT, *messenger for the County Council,*[3] *an old timer*

ANFISA, *nanny, an old woman of 80*

The action takes place in a county seat.[4]

ACT ONE

In the Prozorovs' home. A drawing-room with columns, behind which a large reception room can be seen. Midday: outside it's sunny and bright.[5] In the reception room a table is being set for lunch.

---

2 Chekhov may have taken this unusual name from a well-known family of balalaika players and dancers, who came to prominence in the 1880s.

3 *Zemskaya uprava,* the permanent executive council of the *zemstvo,* or Rural Board, elected from among the members, and not unlike a cabinet in its operations.

4 The capital of the *guberniya* and hence the seat of the regional government.

5 According to V. V. Luzhsky:

In *Three Sisters* on the rise of the curtain, as Stanislavsky's concept has it, birds are singing. These sounds were usually produced by Stanislavsky himself, A. L. Vishnevsky, I. M. Moskvin, V. F. Gribunin, N. G. Aleksandrov, and I, stand-

OLGA, *wearing the dark blue uniform of a teacher at*
a high school for girls,[6] *never stops correcting students'*
examination books, both standing still and on the
move. MASHA, in a black dress, her hat in her lap,
sits reading a book. IRINA, in a white dress, stands
rapt in thought.

OLGA. Father died just a year ago, this very day, the fifth of May, your saint's day,[7] Irina. It was very cold, snowing, in fact. I never thought I'd live through it, you had fainted dead away. But a year's gone by now, and we don't mind thinking about it, you're back to wearing white, your face is beaming. (*The clock strikes twelve.*) The clock struck then too. I remember, when Father was carried to his grave, there was music playing, they fired a salute at the cemetery. He was a general, commanded a whole brigade, but very few people showed up. Of course, it was raining at the time. Pelting rain and snow too.

---

ing in the wings and cooing like doves. [Chekhov] listened to all these she-nanigans, and, walking over to me, said: "Listen, you bill and coo wonderfully, only it's an Egyptian dove!" And of the portrait of the sisters' father—General Prozorov (me in the makeup of an old general) he remarked, "Listen, that's a Japanese general, we don't have that kind in Russia."

(*Solntse Rossii* 228/25 [1914])

6 Olga and Kulygin teach at a *gymnasium*, or four-year high school, open to all classes of society; in 1876, to slow down the upward mobility of the lower classes, a heavy dose of Latin, Greek, and Old Church Slavonic replaced the more dangerous subjects of history, literature, and geography in the extremely rigorous curriculum. Hence Kulygin's frequent citations from the classics.

7 Also known as a name day. Orthodox Russians celebrate the day of the saint after whom a person was named more commonly than they celebrate the person's birthday. St. Irina's day is May 5 in the Orthodox calendar.

IRINA. Why remember?

*Behind the columns, in the reception room near the
table, BARON TUSENBACH, CHEBUTYKIN, and
SOLYONY appear.*

OLGA. Today it's warm, the windows can be thrown open, and the
birch trees aren't even budding yet. Father was put in charge
of a brigade and we all left Moscow eleven years ago, and I distinctly remember, it was early May, why, just this time of year,
everything in Moscow would already be in bloom, warm, everything would be bathed in sunlight. Eleven years have gone by,
but I can remember everything there, as if we'd left yesterday.
Oh my goodness! I woke up this morning, saw the light pour-
ing in, the springtime, and joy began to quicken in my heart, I
began to long passionately for my beloved home.

CHEBUTYKIN. To hell with both of you!

TUSENBACH. You're right, it's ridiculous.

*MASHA, brooding over her book, quietly whistles a
tune under her breath.*[8]

OLGA. Don't whistle, Masha. How can you!

Pause.

---

8 "Don't pull a sorrowful face in any of the acts. Angry, yes, but not sorrowful. People
who go about with inner sorrow a long time and are used to it only whistle and often
grow pensive. So you may every so often grow pensive on stage in the course of the
dialogue" (Chekhov to Olga Knipper, January 2 [15], 1901).

Because I'm at the high school all day long and then have to give tutorials well into the night, I've got this constant headache, and my thoughts are those of an old woman. As a matter of fact, the four years I've been working at the high school, I've felt as if every day my strength and youth were draining from me drop by drop. While that same old dream keeps growing bigger and stronger . . .

IRINA. To go to Moscow. To sell the house, wind up everything here and—go to Moscow . . .

OLGA. Yes! Quick as you can to Moscow.

CHEBUTYKIN and TUSENBACH laugh.

IRINA. Brother will probably become a professor, he certainly won't go on living here. The only thing holding us back is our poor old Masha.

OLGA. Masha will come and spend all summer in Moscow, every year.

MASHA quietly whistles a tune.

IRINA. God willing, everything will work out. (*Looking out the window.*) Lovely weather today. I don't know why my heart feels so light! This morning I remembered that it was my saint's day, and suddenly I felt so happy, and remembered my childhood, when Mama was still alive. And such wonderful thoughts ran through my head, such thoughts!

OLGA. You're simply radiant today, you look especially pretty. And Masha's pretty too. Andrey'd be good looking, only he's putting on too much weight, and it doesn't suit him. And I'm aging just a bit and getting terribly thin, I suppose because I get cross with the girls at school. Well, today I'm free, I'm home, and my head doesn't ache, I feel younger than I did yesterday. I'm only twenty-eight . . . Everything is for the best, everything is God's will, but I do think that if I were married and could stay home all day, things might be better.

Pause.

I'd love my husband.

TUSENBACH (*to Solyony*). You talk such rubbish, a person gets sick and tired just listening to you. (*Entering the drawing-room.*) I forgot to mention. Today you'll be getting a visit from our new battery commander Vershinin. (*Sits at the baby grand piano.*)

OLGA. Is that so? That'll be nice.

IRINA. Is he old?

TUSENBACH. No, not really. Forty at most, forty-five. (*Quietly plays by ear.*) A splendid fellow, by all accounts. And no fool, that's for sure. Only he does talk a lot.

IRINA. Is he interesting?

TUSENBACH. Yes, so-so, but he's got a wife, a mother-in-law, and two little girls. His second wife at that. He goes visiting and tells everybody that he's got a wife and two little girls. He'll tell it here too. The wife's some kind of half-wit, with a long braid, like a schoolgirl, only talks about highfalutin stuff, philosophy, and she makes frequent attempts at suicide, apparently in order to give her husband a hard time. I would have left a woman like that ages ago, but he puts up with it and settles for complaining.

SOLYONY (*entering the drawing-room from the reception room with CHEBUTYKIN*). With one hand I can't lift more than fifty pounds, but with both it goes up to two hundred pounds. Which leads me to conclude that two men are not twice as strong as one, but three times as strong, even stronger . . .

CHEBUTYKIN (*reads the paper as he walks*). For loss of hair . . . eight and a half grams of naphthalene in half a bottle of grain alcohol . . . dissolve and apply daily . . .[9] (*Makes a note in a memo book.*) Let's jot that down, shall we! (*To Solyony.*) Listen, as I was saying, you stick a tiny little cork in a tiny little bottle, and pass a tiny little glass tube through it . . . Then you take a tiny little pinch of the most common, ordinary alum . . .

IRINA. Ivan Romanych, dear Ivan Romanych!

CHEBUTYKIN. What, my darling girl, light of my life?

IRINA. Tell me, why am I so happy today? I feel as if I'm skimming along at full sail, with the wide blue sky above me and big white birds drifting by. Why is that? Why?

---

9 Letter of Olga Knipper to Chekhov (September 12, 1900): "I'm going to give you a wonderful remedy to keep hair from falling out. Take ½ bottle of methylated spirits and mix in 8 grams of naphtalin and rub it in regularly—it's a big help. Will you do it? Because it's not a good idea to come to Moscow bald—people will think I pulled your hair out."

CHEBUTYKIN (*kissing both her hands, tenderly*). My own white bird . . .

IRINA. When I woke up today, I got out of bed and washed, and suddenly it dawned on me that I understand everything in the world and I know how a person ought to live. Dear Ivan Romanych, I know everything. A person has to work hard, work by the sweat of his brow, no matter who he is, and that's the only thing that gives meaning and purpose to his life, his happiness, his moments of ecstasy. Wouldn't it be wonderful to be a manual laborer who gets up while it's still dark out and breaks stones on the road, or a shepherd, or a schoolteacher, or an engineer on the railroad . . . My God, what's the point of being human, you might as well be an ox, an ordinary horse, so long as you're working, rather than a young woman who gets up at noon, has her coffee in bed, and takes two hours to dress . . . oh, isn't that awful! Sometimes when the weather's sultry, the way you long for a drink, well, that's the way I long for work. And if I don't get up early and work hard, stop being my friend, Ivan Romanych.

CHEBUTYKIN (*tenderly*). I will, I will . . .

OLGA. Father drilled us to get up at seven. Nowadays Irina wakes up at seven and stays in bed at least till nine, thinking about things. And the serious face on her! (*Laughs.*)

IRINA. You're used to treating me like a little girl, so you think it's strange when I put on a serious face. I'm twenty years old!

TUSENBACH. The longing for hard work, oh dear, how well I understand it! I've never worked in my life. I was born in Petersburg, cold, idle Petersburg, to a family that didn't know the meaning of hard work or hardship. I remember, whenever I came home from school, a lackey would pull off my boots, while I'd fidget and my mother would gaze at me in adoration and be surprised when anyone looked at me any other way. They tried to shield me from hard work. And they just about managed it, only just! The time has come, there's a thundercloud looming over us, there's a bracing, mighty tempest lying in wait, close at hand, and soon it will blow all the indolence, apathy, prejudice against hard work, putrid boredom out of our society. I shall work, and in twenty-five or thirty years everyone will be working. Every last one of us!

CHEBUTYKIN. I won't work.

TUSENBACH. You don't count.

SOLYONY. In twenty-five years you won't be on this earth, thank God. In two or three years you'll die of apoplexy, or I'll fly off the handle and put a bullet through your brain, angel mine. (*Takes a flask of perfume from his pocket and sprinkles his chest and hands.*)

CHEBUTYKIN (*laughs*). As a matter of fact, I've never done a thing. Ever since I left the university, I haven't lifted a finger, not even read a book, nothing but newspapers . . . (*Takes from his pocket a second newspaper.*) You see . . . I know by the papers that there was, let's say, somebody named Dobrolyubov,[10] but what he wrote—I don't know . . . God knows . . . (*Someone can be heard knocking on the floor from a lower story.*) There . . . They're calling for me downstairs, someone's come for me. I'll be right there . . . hold on . . . . (*Leaves hurriedly, combing his beard.*)

IRINA. This is something he's cooked up.

TUSENBACH. Yes. He went out with a look of triumph on his face, I'll bet he's about to deliver a present.

IRINA. How unpleasant!

OLGA. Yes, it's awful. He's always doing something silly.

MASHA. "On the curved seashore a green oak stands, a golden chain wound round that oak . . . A golden chain wound round that oak . . ."[11] (*Rises and hums quietly.*)

OLGA. You're in a funny mood today, Masha. (*MASHA, humming, adjusts her hat.*) Where are you off to?

MASHA. Home.

IRINA. Strange . . .

---

10 Nikolay Aleksandrovich Dobrolyubov (1836–1861), Russian journalist of the radical democratic camp and proponent of realistic literature. He invented the concept of the "superfluous man."

11 Masha is quoting from the opening lines of the famous poetic fable *Ruslan and Lyudmila*, by Aleksandr Pushkin, a classic love story. On her wedding night, Lyudmila is abducted by a wizard and Ruslan finds her only after many adventures. The lines are: "On the curved seashore a green oak stands, / A golden chain wound round that oak; / And night and day a learned cat / Walks round and round upon that chain. / When he goes right a song he sings, / When he goes left a tale he tells." An English equivalent might be Edward Lear's "The owl and the pussy-cat went to sea, In a beautiful pea-green boat . . . A beautiful pea-green boat . . ."

TUSENBACH. Leaving a saint's day party!

MASHA. Doesn't matter . . . I'll be back this evening. Good-bye, my dearest . . . (*Kisses Irina.*) Best wishes once more, good health, be happy. In the old days, when Father was alive, every time we celebrated a saint's day some thirty or forty officers would show up, there was lots of noise, but today there's only a man and a half, and it's as desolate as a desert . . . I'm off . . . I'm melancholeric[12] today, I don't feel very cheerful, and you musn't mind me. (*Laughs through tears.*) Later we'll have a talk, but good-bye for now, my darling, I'm off.

IRINA (*put out*). Well, that's just like you . . .

OLGA (*plaintively*). I understand you, Masha.

SOLYONY. If a man philosophizes, you could call it philosophistry or even sophisticuffs, but if a woman philosophizes or two women, that you could call — Polly want a cracker!

MASHA. What do you mean by that, you dreadfully awful man?

SOLYONY. Not a thing. "He scarcely had time to gasp, When the bear had him in its grasp."[13]

---

12 *Merlekhyundiya*, instead of *melankholiya*. A favorite word of Chekhov's, often used in private correspondence, as well as in "The Examining Magistrate" and *Ivanov*. " . . . your nerves are in bad shape and you're under the sway of a psychiatric semi-ailment, which seminarians call melancholera" (to A. A. Suvorin, August 23, 1893).

13 Quotation from the fable "The Peasant and the Farmhand," by Ivan Krylov (1768–1844), which Chekhov also quotes in the story "Among Friends" (1898): "He had a habit, unsettling for his interlocutor, of pronouncing as an exclamation a certain phrase which had no relation to the conversation, while snapping his fingers."

Pause.

MASHA (*to Olga, angrily*). Stop sniveling!

Enter ANFISA and FERAPONT with a layer cake.

ANFISA. Over here, dearie. Come on in, your feet're clean. (*To Irina.*) From the County Council, from Protopopov, from Mikhail Ivanych . . . A cake.

IRINA. Thank you. Thank him. (*Takes the cake.*)

FERAPONT. How's that?

IRINA (*louder*). Thank him!

OLGA. Nanny dear, give him some pie. Ferapont, go on, out there they'll give you some pie.

FERAPONT. How's that?

ANFISA. Let's go, dearie, Ferapont Spiridonych. Let's go . . . (*Exits with FERAPONT.*)

MASHA. I do not like Protopopov, that bear bearing gifts. It isn't right to invite him.

IRINA. I didn't invite him.

MASHA. Good girl.

Enter CHEBUTYKIN, followed by a soldier carrying a silver samovar; a low murmur of astonishment and displeasure.

OLGA (*hides her face in her hands*). A samovar! How dreadfully inappropriate.[14] (*Goes to the table in the reception room.*)

IRINA. Ivan Romanych, you darling, what are you doing!

TUSENBACH (*laughs*). I told you so. — *Together*

MASHA. Ivan Romanych, you're simply shameless!

CHEBUTYKIN. My dears, my darlings, you're the only ones I have, for me you're more precious than anything on this earth. I'll be sixty soon, I'm an old man, a lonely, insignificant old man . . . There's nothing good about me, except this love for you, and if it weren't for you, I'd be dead and gone long ago . . . (*To Irina.*) My dearest child, I've known you since the day you were born . . . I held you in my arms . . . I loved your poor mama . . .

IRINA. But why such expensive presents?

CHEBUTYKIN (*through tears, angrily*). Expensive presents . . . You're the limit! (*To the orderly.*) Put the samovar over there . . . (*Mimics.*) Expensive presents . . . (*The orderly takes the samovar into the reception room.*)

ANFISA (*crossing the drawing-room*). My dears, a strange colonel! He's already took off his overcoat, boys and girls, he's com-

---

14 A samovar was traditionally given by a husband to his wife on their silver or golden anniversary.

ing in here. Arinushka, now you be a charming, polite little girl . . . (*Going out.*) Lunch should have been served a long time ago now . . . Honest to goodness . . .

TUSENBACH. Vershinin, I suppose.

Enter VERSHININ.

Lieutenant Colonel Vershinin.

VERSHININ (*to Masha and Irina*). May I introduce myself: Vershinin.[15] Very, very pleased to meet you at long last. How you've grown! My! my!

IRINA. Do sit down, please. We're glad to have you.

VERSHININ (*merrily*). I am delighted, delighted. But weren't you three sisters? I remember three little girls. I've stopped remembering faces, but your father, Colonel Prozorov, had three little girls, that I distinctly remember and I saw them with my own eyes. How time flies. Dear, dear, how time flies!

TUSENBACH. The Colonel is from Moscow.

IRINA. From Moscow? You're from Moscow?

VERSHININ. Yes, that's where I'm from. Your late father was battery commander there, I was an officer in the same brigade. (*To Masha.*) Now your face I do seem to remember.

---

15 "When I played Vershinin, Chekhov said: 'Good, very good. Only don't salute like that, it's not like a colonel. You salute like a lieutenant. You have to do it more firmly, more confidently' " (Vasily Kachalov, *Shipovnik Almanac* 23 [1914]).

MASHA. And I remember yours—not at all!

IRINA. Olya! Olya! (*Shouts into the reception room.*) Olya, come here! (*OLGA enters the drawing-room from the reception room.*) Lieutenant Colonel Vershinin, it turns out, is from Moscow.

VERSHININ. You must be Olga Sergeevna, the eldest . . . And you're Masha . . . And you're Irina—the youngest . . .

OLGA. You're from Moscow?

VERSHININ. Yes. I was at school in Moscow and entered the service in Moscow, served a long time there, was finally assigned a battery here—I've been transferred here, as you see. I don't remember you individually, I only remember that you were three sisters. Your father's stuck in my memory, why, I can close my eyes and see him as if he were alive. I used to visit you in Moscow . . .

OLGA. I was sure I remembered everyone, and suddenly . . .

VERSHININ. My name is Aleksandr Ignatyevich . . .

IRINA. Aleksandr Ignatyevich, you're from Moscow . . . That's a coincidence!

OLGA. In fact we'll be moving there.

IRINA. We think we'll be there as soon as autumn. Our home town, we were born there . . . On Old Basmanny Street . . .

Both women laugh for joy.

MASHA. We've unexpectedly come across someone from our neck of the woods! (*Vivaciously.*) Now I remember! I do remember.

Olya, at home they used to talk about "the lovesick major." You were a lieutenant then and in love with someone, and everybody teased you, calling you major for some reason . . .

VERSHININ (*laughs*). That's right, that's right! . . . The lovesick major, right you are . . .

MASHA. Then you only had a moustache . . . Oh, how you've aged! (*Plaintively.*) How you've aged!

VERSHININ. Yes, in those days they called me the lovesick major, I was still young and in love. It's not the same now.

OLGA. But you don't have a single gray hair yet. You've aged, but you haven't grown old.

VERSHININ. Nevertheless I am forty-three. Have you been away from Moscow a long time?

IRINA. Eleven years. Why, what's wrong, Masha, you're crying, you crazy . . . (*Plaintively.*) Now I'm starting to cry . . .

MASHA. I'm all right. And what street did you live on?

VERSHININ. Old Basmanny.

OLGA. Why, we lived there too . . .

VERSHININ. At one time I lived on German Street. I'd walk from German Street to the Red Barracks. On the way there's this grim-looking bridge, with the water roaring beneath it. A lonely man begins to feel his heart bowed down.

Pause.

But here there's such a broad, such a fertile river! A wonderful river!

OLGA. Yes, only it's cold. It's cold here and there are mosquitoes . . .

VERSHININ. Why should you care? Here there's such a wholesome, bracing Russian climate. A forest, a river . . . and birch trees here too. Dear, humble birches, I love them more than any other tree. It's a good place to live. Only it's odd, the train station is over thirteen miles away . . . And nobody knows why that is.

SOLYONY. I know why that is. (*Everyone stares at him.*) Because if the station were nearby, it wouldn't be far away, and if it were far away, obviously it wouldn't be nearby.

An awkward silence.

TUSENBACH. Always clowning, Solyony.

OLGA. Now I've remembered you too. I do remember.

VERSHININ. I knew your dear mother.

CHEBUTYKIN. She was a good woman, rest her soul.

IRINA. Mama is buried in Moscow.

OLGA. In Novo-devichy churchyard . . .[16]

---

16 Graveyard attached to the historic Moscow "New Virgin" convent, where many celebrities of politics, society, and culture, including Chekhov and his father, are buried.

MASHA. Just imagine, I'm already beginning to forget what she looked like. No one will remember about us either. They'll forget.

VERSHININ. Yes. They'll forget. Such is our fate, nothing you can do about it. The things we take to be serious, meaningful, of great importance—a time will come when they will be forgotten or seem of no importance.

Pause.

And the interesting thing is, we have absolutely no way of knowing just what will be considered sublime and important, and what trivial and absurd. Didn't the discoveries of Copernicus or, say, Columbus at first sound pointless, absurd, while some idiotic nonsense written by a crank sounded true? And it may come about that our present life, which we're so used to, will in time seem strange, uncomfortable, unintelligent, devoid of purity, maybe even depraved . . .

TUSENBACH. Who knows? Maybe they'll call our life elevated and remember us with respect. Nowadays we don't have torture, executions, invasions, and yet there's so much suffering.

SOLYONY (*shrilly*). Cheep, cheep, cheep . . . Don't feed the Baron birdseed, just let 'im philosophize.

TUSENBACH. Solyony, please leave me in peace . . . (*Moves to another seat.*) It gets to be a bore, after a while.

SOLYONY (*shrilly*). Cheep, cheep, cheep . . .

TUSENBACH (*to Vershinin*). The suffering that's so conspicuous nowadays—and there's so much of it!—nevertheless betokens a certain moral progress which society has already achieved . . .

VERSHININ. Yes, yes, of course.

CHEBUTYKIN. You said just now, Baron, they'll call our life elevated, but all the same people are low . . . (*Rises.*) Look how low I am. My only consolation is you telling me my life is elevated and makes sense.

Offstage someone is playing a violin.

MASHA. That's Andrey playing, our brother.

IRINA. He's the scholar of the family. He's meant to be a professor. Papa was a military man, but his son chose an academic career.

MASHA. As Papa wished.

OLGA. Today we were teasing the life out of him. He's a bit infatuated, it seems.

IRINA. With a certain local miss. She'll show up here today, most likely.

MASHA. Ah, the way she dresses! It's not so much unbecoming or unfashionable as simply pathetic. Some strange, gaudy, yellowish skirt with a vulgar little fringe and a red jacket. And her cheeks are scrubbed so raw! Andrey is not in love—I won't allow that, after all he has taste, but he's simply, well, teasing us, playing the fool. Yesterday I heard she's marrying Protopopov, the chairman of the County Council. And a good thing too . . . (*Out the side door.*) Andrey, come here! Just for a second, dear!

Enter ANDREY.

OLGA. This is my brother, Andrey Sergeich.

VERSHININ. Vershinin.

ANDREY. Prozorov. (*Wipes his sweating face.*) You're here as battery commander?

OLGA. Imagine, the Colonel is from Moscow.

ANDREY. Really? Well, congratulations, now my sisters won't give you a moment's peace.

VERSHININ. I've had plenty of time already to bore your sisters.

IRINA. Just look at the portrait-frame Andrey gave me today! (*Displays the frame.*) He made it himself.

VERSHININ (*looking at the frame and not knowing what to say*). Yes . . . quite something . . .

IRINA. And there's that picture frame over the baby grand, he made that too.

ANDREY waves his hand in dismissal and moves away.

OLGA. He's the scholar in the family and plays the violin and makes all sorts of things with his fretsaw, in short, a jack-of-all-trades. Andrey, don't go away! He's funny that way—always wandering off. Come over here!

MASHA and IRINA take him by the arms and laughingly escort him back.

MASHA. Come on, come on!

ANDREY. Leave me alone, for pity's sake.

MASHA. Don't be ridiculous! They used to call the Colonel the lovesick major and he didn't get the tiniest bit angry.

VERSHININ. Not the tiniest bit!

MASHA. And I want to call you: the lovesick fiddler!

IRINA. Or the lovesick professor! . . .

OLGA. He's lovesick! Andryusha's lovesick!

IRINA (*applauding*). Bravo, bravo! Encore! Little Andryusha's lovesick!

CHEBUTYKIN (*comes up behind Andrey and puts both arms around his waist*). "For love alone did Nature put us on this earth!"[17] (*Roars with laughter: he's still holding on to his newspaper.*)

ANDREY. All right, that's enough, that's enough . . . (*Wipes his face.*) I didn't get a wink of sleep last night and now I'm not

---

17 The opening of Taisiya's "Russian aria" in the old opera-vaudeville *Reversals* by Pyotr Kobryakov (1808): "For love alone did Nature / Put us on this earth; / As comfort to the mortal race / She gave the gift of tender feelings!"

quite myself, as they say. I read until four, then I went to bed, but it was no good. I kept thinking about this and that, and the next thing I knew it's dawn and the sun's creeping into my bedroom. This summer, while I'm still here, I want to translate a certain book from the English.

VERSHININ. So you read English?

ANDREY. Yes. Father, rest in peace, overstocked us with education. It sounds silly and absurd, but, still, I must admit, after his death I started putting on weight and, well, I put on so much weight in one year, it's as if my body were freeing itself of its constraints. Thanks to Father, my sisters and I know French, German, and English, and Irina also knows a little Italian. But what good is it?

MASHA. In this town knowing three languages is a superfluous luxury. Not even a luxury, but a kind of superfluous appendage, a bit like a sixth finger. We know a lot of useless stuff.

VERSHININ. Well, I'll be. (*Laughs.*) I don't think there is or can be a town so boring and dismal that an intelligent, educated person isn't of use. Let's assume that among the one hundred thousand inhabitants of this town, which is, I grant you, backward and crude, there are only three such as you. Naturally, it's not up to you to enlighten the benighted masses that surround you. In the course of your lifetime you must gradually surrender and be swallowed up in the crowd of a hundred thousand, you'll be smothered by life, but even so you won't disappear,

[90]

won't sink without a trace. In your wake others like you will appear, maybe six, then twelve, and so on, until at last the likes of you will be the majority. In two hundred, three hundred years life on earth will be unimaginably beautiful, stupendous. Man needs a life like that, and if it isn't here and now, then he must look forward to it, wait, dream, prepare himself for it, and that's the reason he must see and know more than his father and grandfather saw and knew. (*Laughs.*) And you complain you know a lot of useless stuff.

MASHA (*takes off her hat*). I'm staying for lunch.

IRINA (*with a sigh*). Honestly, I should have taken notes . . .

ANDREY's gone, he left unnoticed.

TUSENBACH. Many years from now, you say, life on earth will be beautiful, stupendous. That's true. But to take part in it now, even remotely, a person has to prepare for it, a person has to work . . .

VERSHININ (*rises*). Yes. By the way, you have so many flowers! (*Looking around.*) And wonderful quarters! I'm jealous! All my life I've knocked around in cramped quarters with two chairs, the same old sofa, and stoves that invariably smoke. The main thing missing in my life has been flowers like these . . . (*Waves his hand in dismissal.*) Oh, well! That's how it is!

TUSENBACH. Yes, a person has to work. I suppose you're thinking: he's gushing all over the place like a typical sentimental

German.[18] But, word of honor, I'm a Russian, I don't even speak German. My father belongs to the Orthodox Church . . .

Pause.

VERSHININ (*paces the stage back and forth*). I often think: what if a man were to begin life anew, and fully conscious at that? If one life, which has already been lived out, were, how shall I put it?, a rough draft, and the other—a final revision! Then each of us, I think, would, first of all, try hard not to repeat himself, at least we'd create a different setting for our life, we'd furnish quarters like these for ourselves with flowers, great bunches of flowers . . . I have a wife, two little girls, moreover my wife's not a well woman, et cetera, et cetera, yes, but if one were to begin life from the beginning, I wouldn't get married . . . No, no!

Enter KULYGIN in a uniform dresscoat.[19]

KULYGIN (*comes up to Irina*). Dearest sister, may I congratulate you on your saint's day and sincerely wish you, from the bottom of my heart, the best of health and all those things proper to wish a young girl of your years. (*Gives her a book.*) The history of our high school over the past fifty years, written by yours truly. A frivolous little book, written when I had nothing better to do, but you go ahead and read it all the same. Greetings,

18 Tusenbach further explains his German ancestry in Act Two. In Chekhov's notebooks, Tusenbach's patronymic is Karlovich (son of Karl), which was later changed to Lvovich (son of Leo, a more Russian name).

19 "You wear the tailcoat only in Act One; as to the bandolier (a polished black strap) you are quite right. At least until Act Four you should wear the uniform such as it was before 1900" (Chekhov to Aleksandr Vishnevsky, January 6 [18], 1901).

ladies and gentlemen! (*To Vershinin.*) Kulygin, teacher in the local high school. Civil servant, seventh class. (*To Irina.*) In that book you'll find a list of all the alumni of our high school for the past fifty years. *Feci quod potui, faciant meliora potentes.*[20] (*Kisses Masha.*)

IRINA. But didn't you give me this book last Easter?

KULYGIN (*laughs*). Impossible! In that case give it back, or better yet, give it to the Colonel. Here you are, Colonel. Some day you'll read it when you're bored.

VERSHININ. Thank you. (*Prepares to go.*) I'm most happy to have made your acquaintance . . .

OLGA. You're going? No, no!

IRINA. You'll stay and have lunch with us. Please.

OLGA. I insist!

VERSHININ (*bows*). I seem to have dropped in on a saint's day party. Forgive me, I didn't know, I haven't congratulated you . . . (*Goes into the reception room with OLGA.*)

KULYGIN. Today, ladies and gentlemen, is Sunday, the day of rest, therefore let us rest, let us make merry each according to his age and station in life. The rugs will have to be taken up for summer and put away until winter . . . With moth balls or

---

20 Latin: I have done what I could, let those who can do better. A paraphrase of Cicero, when the Roman consulate conferred his powers on his successors.

naphthalene . . . The Romans were a healthy people because they knew how to work hard and they knew how to relax, they had *mens sana in corpore sano*.[21] Their life moved according to a set pattern. Our headmaster says: the main thing in every man's life is its pattern . . . Whatever loses its pattern ceases to exist— and in our everyday life the same holds true. (*Takes Masha round the waist, laughing.*) Masha loves me. My wife loves me. And the window curtains too along with the rugs . . . Today I'm cheerful, in splendid spirits. Masha, at four o'clock today we have to go to the headmaster's. An outing's been arranged for the faculty and their families.

MASHA. I'm not going.

KULYGIN (*mortified*). Masha dear, whyever not?

MASHA. We'll discuss it later . . . (*Angrily.*) Very well, I'll go, but do leave me alone, for pity's sake . . . (*Walks away.*)

KULYGIN. And then we'll spend the evening at the headmaster's. Despite his failing health that man strives above all to be sociable. An outstanding, brilliant personality. A magnificent man. Yesterday after our meeting he says to me, "I'm tired, Fyodor Ilyich! I'm tired!" (*Looks at the clock on the wall, then at his watch.*) Your clock is seven minutes fast. Yes, says he, I'm tired!

Offstage someone is playing the violin.

---

21 Latin: "A healthy mind in a healthy body," quotation from the *Satires* of Juvenal.

OLGA. Ladies and gentlemen, please come to the table! There's a meat pie!

KULYGIN. Ah, my dear Olga, my dear! Yesterday I worked from morn to eleven at night, I was exhausted and today I feel happy. (*Goes to the table in the reception room.*) My dear . . .

CHEBUTYKIN (*puts the newspaper in his pocket, combs out his beard*). A meat pie? Splendid!

MASHA (*sternly, to Chebutykin*). Just watch your step, don't have anything to drink today. You hear? Drinking's bad for you.

CHEBUTYKIN. Bah! That's over and done with. Two years since I last was drunk. (*Impatiently.*) Anyways, lady, it don't make no never mind!

MASHA. All the same don't you dare drink. Don't you dare. (*Angrily, but so her husband can't hear.*) Damn it to hell, another boring evening at the headmaster's!

TUSENBACH. If I were in your shoes, I wouldn't go . . . Plain and simple.

CHEBUTYKIN. Don't go, my lovely!

MASHA. 'S all very well to say: don't go . . . This damned life is unbearable . . . (*Goes into the reception room.*)

CHEBUTYKIN (*following her*). Now, now!

SOLYONY (*crossing into the reception room*). Cheep, cheep, cheep . . .

TUSENBACH. That's enough, Solyony. Cut it out!

SOLYONY. Cheep, cheep, cheep . . .

KULYGIN (*merrily*). Your health, Colonel! I'm an educator, and here in this house one of the family, Masha's hubby . . . She's a kindhearted creature, really kind . . .

VERSHININ. I'll have some of that dark vodka[22] there . . . (*Drinks.*) Your health! (*To Olga.*) I feel so good being here with you! . . .

In the drawing-room IRINA and TUSENBACH remain.

IRINA. Masha's in a funny mood today. She married at eighteen, when he seemed to her to be the cleverest of men. And now he doesn't. He's the kindest, but not the cleverest.

OLGA (*impatiently*). Andrey, are you coming?

ANDREY (*offstage*). Right away. (*Enters and goes to the table.*)

TUSENBACH. What are you thinking about?

IRINA. This. I don't like that Solyony of yours, I'm afraid of him. Everything he says is stupid . . .

TUSENBACH. He's a strange fellow. I feel sorry for him, and I get annoyed by him, but mostly sorry. I think he's shy . . . When we're alone together, he's often clever and pleasant enough, but in company he's rude, a bully. Don't go, let them sit at

---

22 Vodka is traditionally flavored with herbs and spices, such as buffalo grass, cardamom, and peppercorns.

the table a little. Let me be near you for a while. What are you thinking about? (*Pause.*) You're twenty, I'm not yet thirty. How many years there are ahead of us, a long, long series of days, filled with my love for you . . .

IRINA. Nikolay Lvovich, don't talk to me about love . . .

TUSENBACH (*not listening*). I thirst so passionately for life, struggle, hard work, and this thirst of my heart has blended with my love of you, Irina, and it all seems to fit, because you're beautiful and life looks just as beautiful to me! What are you thinking about?

IRINA. You say: life is beautiful. Yes, but what if it only seems that way! For us three sisters, life hasn't been beautiful, it's choked us, like weeds . . . There are tears running down my face. That's not what we need . . . (*Quickly wipes her face, smiles.*) What we need is work, work. That's why things look so gloomy to us, why we take such a dim view of life, because we don't know what hard work is. We're the children of people who despised hard work . . .

> NATALIYA IVANOVNA *enters, wearing a pink dress*
> *with a green belt.*

NATASHA.[23] They've already sat down to lunch . . . I'm late . . . (*Catches a glimpse of herself in a mirror, sets herself to rights.*) My hairdo looks all right . . . (*On seeing Irina.*) Dear Irina Sergeevna, congratulations! (*Kisses her energetically and*

---

23 "Natasha" is the usual diminutive of "Nataliya" and is used throughout by the sisters.

at length.) You've got a lot of guests, honestly, I'm embarrassed . . . Good afternoon, Baron!

OLGA (*entering the drawing-room*). Why, here's Nataliya Ivanovna too. Good afternoon, my dear!

They exchange kisses.

NATASHA. With the party girl. You've got such a lot of company, I'm awfully nervous . . .

OLGA. Don't be silly, it's all family. (*In an undertone, shocked.*) You're wearing a green belt! My dear, that's a mistake!

NATASHA. Is it bad luck?

OLGA. No, it simply doesn't go . . . It's all wrong somehow . . .

NATASHA (*on the verge of tears*). Really? But actually it's not green, it's more a sort of beige.

Follows OLGA into the reception room. In the reception room everyone is seated at the table; not a soul is left in the drawing-room.

KULYGIN. I wish you, Irina, a proper fiancé. It's high time you got married.

CHEBUTYKIN. Nataliya Ivanovna, I wish you a tiny little fiancé.

KULYGIN. Nataliya Ivanovna already has a tiny little fiancé.

MASHA (*raps a fork on a plate*). I'll have a glass of wine! What the hell, life's for living, so let's live dangerously!

KULYGIN. Your conduct gets C minus.

VERSHININ. My, this is a tasty cordial. What's it flavored with?

SOLYONY. Cockroaches.

IRINA (*on the verge of tears*). Ick! Ick! That's disgusting! . . .

OLGA. For supper we're having roast turkey and apple pie.[24] Thank God, I'm home all day today, home this evening . . . Gentlemen, do come again this evening.

VERSHININ. May I come in the evening too?

IRINA. Please do.

NATASHA. It's do as you please around here.

CHEBUTYKIN. "For love alone did Nature put us on this earth." (*Laughs.*)

ANDREY (*angrily*). Will you stop it, gentlemen! Don't you get sick of it?

FEDOTIK and RODÉ enter with a large basket
of flowers.

FEDOTIK. They're already eating lunch.

RODÉ (*loudly, rolling his rs*). They're already eating? Yes, they are already eating . . .

---

24 American though this sounds, the turkey would have been stuffed with liver and walnuts, sliced, and served with a Madeira sauce. The open-face apple pie would contain almonds, cherry jam, and raisins.

FEDOTIK. Wait just a minute! (*Takes a snapshot.*) One! Hold it just a bit more . . . (*Takes another snapshot.*) Two! Now we're through!

> They take the basket and go into the reception room,
> where they are greeted boisterously.

RODÉ (*loudly*). Congratulations, I wish you the best of everything, the best of everything! Enchanting weather today, simply splendid. All this morning I was out on a hike with the high school students. I teach gymnastics at the high school . . .

FEDOTIK. You may move now, Irina Sergeevna, yes you may! (*Takes a snapshot.*) You are an interesting model today. (*Pulls a humming-top out of his pocket.*) And in addition, look, a humming-top . . . Makes a wonderful sound . . .

IRINA. What a treasure!

MASHA. "On the curved seashore a green oak stands, a golden chain wound round that oak . . . A golden chain wound round that oak . . ." (*Tearfully.*) Now, why do I keep saying that? Those lines have been stuck in my head since this morning . . .

KULYGIN. Thirteen at table!

RODÉ (*loudly*). Ladies and gentlemen, how can you possibly lend credence to superstitions?

> Laughter.

KULYGIN. If there are thirteen at table, that means there are lovers here. Might you be one, Doctor, perish the thought . . .

Laughter.

CHEBUTYKIN. I've been a sinner from way back, but, look, why Nataliya Ivanovna should get embarrassed is something I simply cannot understand.

Loud laughter. NATASHA runs out of the reception room into the drawing-room, followed by ANDREY.

ANDREY. Never mind, don't pay any attention! Wait . . . Stop, please . . .

NATASHA. I'm embarrassed . . . I don't know what to do with myself, and they're all poking fun at me. I just left the table, and I know it's impolite, but I can't . . . I can't . . . (*Hides her face in her hands.*)

ANDREY. My dearest, please, I beg you, don't get upset. I swear to you, they're only joking, it's all in good fun. My dearest, my own, they're all kind, loving people, and they love me and you. Come over here to the window where they can't see us . . . (*Looking around.*)

NATASHA. I'm so unaccustomed to being in society! . . .

ANDREY. Oh, youth, wonderful, beautiful youth. My dearest, my own, don't get so upset! . . . Believe me, believe me . . . I feel so good, my heart is brimming over with love, delight . . . Oh, they can't see us! They can't see! Why I fell in love with you, when I fell in love with you—oh, I have no idea. My dearest, good, pure love, be my wife! I'd love you, love you . . . like no one ever . . . (*A kiss.*)

TWO OFFICERS enter and, on seeing the kissing
couple, stop in amazement.

Curtain

ACT TWO

Same set as in Act One.

Eight o'clock at night. From offstage, as if from the
street, one can faintly hear a concertina playing.
No lights.

Enter NATALIYA IVANOVNA in a housecoat and
carrying a candle; she walks around and stops by the
door leading to Andrey's room.

NATASHA. Andryusha, what're you doing? Reading? Never mind,
I'm just . . . (*Walks around, opens another door and, after peep-*
ing in, closes it again.) Seeing if there's a light . . .

ANDREY (*enters, holding a book*). You what, Natasha?

NATASHA. I'm checking to see if there's a light . . . Now that it's
carnival week,[25] the servants are out of control, you have to

---

25 *Maslennitsa*, or Butter Week, the week preceding Lent, was traditionally devoted
to eating and carousing. The consumption of pancakes (*blini*) and the invitation of
musicians into homes were traditional activities. Evidently a year and nine months
have passed since Act One.

keep a sharp lookout to see that nothing goes wrong. Last night at midnight I was walking through the dining room and there was a candle burning. Who lit it, I never did manage to find out. (*Puts down the candle.*) What time is it?

ANDREY (*after a look at his watch*). Quarter past eight.

NATASHA. And Olga and Irina not back yet. They aren't here. Still at work, poor things. Olga at the faculty meeting, Irina at the telegraph office . . . (*Sighs.*) Just this morning I was saying to your sister, "Take care of yourself," I say, "Irina, love." But she doesn't listen. A quarter past eight, you said? I'm worried our Bobik[26] isn't at all well. Why is he so cold? Yesterday he had a fever and today he's cold all over . . . I'm so worried!

ANDREY. It's nothing, Natasha. The boy's healthy.

NATASHA. But even so we'd better put him on a diet. I'm worried. And at nine o'clock tonight, they were saying, the masqueraders[27] will be here. It'd be better if they didn't put in an appearance, Andryusha.

ANDREY. I really don't know. After all, they were sent for.

NATASHA. This morning the little darling woke up and looks at me, and suddenly he smiled, which means he recognized me.

---

26 Natasha is being pretentious but gets it wrong. An English name such as Bob was fashionable in high society, but at this time Bobik was usually applied to dogs.

27 *Ryazhenye* were well-behaved amateur performers in carnival costume who, after dusk, would go from house to house at Shrovetide, dancing and receiving food in return. Trick-or-treaters and carolers combined, they might be joined by professional bear leaders, storytellers, and beggars. For a description, see Tolstoy's *War and Peace*, II, part 4, ch. 10.

"Bobik," I say, "morning! morning! darling!" And he laughs. Children do understand, they understand perfectly well. So, in that case, Andryusha, I'll tell the servants not to let the masqueraders in.

ANDREY (*indecisively*). But, after all, that's up to my sisters. They're in charge here.

NATASHA. Oh, they are too, I'll tell them. They're considerate . . . (*Walks around.*) For supper I ordered some yogurt. Doctor says you shouldn't eat anything but yogurt, otherwise you won't lose weight. (*Stops.*) Bobik is cold. I'm worried, it's too cold for him in his room, most likely. At least until the weather gets warmer we should put him in another room. For instance, Irina's room is just right for a baby, it's dry and sunny all day long. I'll have to tell her, meanwhile she can double up with Olga in the same room . . . It doesn't matter, she's not at home during the day, only spends the night here . . . (*Pause.*) Andryusha sweetie-pie, why don't you say something?

ANDREY. No reason, I was thinking . . . Besides there's nothing to be said . . .

NATASHA. Right . . . Something I wanted to tell you . . . Oh, yes. Ferapont's out there, sent by the council, he's asking to see you.

ANDREY (*yawns*). Send him in.

> NATASHA *exits*; ANDREY, *hunched over the candle she's forgotten, reads a book. Enter* FERAPONT; *he is wearing an old threadbare overcoat with a turned-up collar, his ears covered by a kerchief.*

ANDREY. 'Evening, old-timer. What have you got to say for yourself?

FERAPONT. Chairman sent a book and a paper of some sort. Here . . . (*Hands over a book and a paper.*)

ANDREY. Thanks. Fine. But why didn't you get here earlier? After all, it's past eight already.

FERAPONT. How's that?

ANDREY (*Louder*). I said, you've come so late, it's already past eight.

FERAPONT. Right you are. When I got here it was still light, but they wouldn't let me in all this time. The master, they say, is busy. Well, that's that. Busy's busy, I got no cause to rush. (*Thinking that Andrey is asking him something.*) How's that?

ANDREY. Nothing. (*Examining the book.*) Tomorrow's Friday, we don't meet, but I'll go there all the same . . . I'll find something to do, it's boring at home . . .

Pause.

You dear old man, it's funny the way things change, the way life isn't fair! Today out of boredom, with nothing to do, I picked up this book here—my old university lecture notes, and I had to laugh . . . Good grief, I'm secretary to the County Council, the council Protopopov presides over, I'm secretary and the most I can hope for—is to become a full member of the County Council! Me a member of the local County Council, me, who dreams every night that I'm a professor at Moscow University, a famous scholar, the pride of Russia!

FERAPONT. I couldn't say . . . I'm hard o' hearing . . .

ANDREY. If your hearing was good, I probably wouldn't be talking to you. I have to talk to someone, and my wife doesn't understand me, my sisters scare me for some reason, I'm afraid they'll make fun of me, embarrass me . . . I don't drink, I've no great fondness for barrooms, but I'd love to be sitting in Moscow at Testov's tavern right now or the Grand Moscow restaurant, my friend.

FERAPONT. Why, in Moscow, a contractor at the Council was saying the other day, there was some shopkeepers eating pancakes;[28] one ate forty pancakes and like to died. May ha' been forty, may ha' been fifty. I don't rec'llect.

ANDREY. You sit in Moscow in the vast main dining room of a restaurant, you don't know anyone and no one knows you, and at the same time you don't feel like a stranger. Whereas here you know everyone and everyone knows you, but you're a stranger, a stranger . . . A stranger and alone.

FERAPONT. How's that?

Pause.

And that same contractor was saying—lying too, mebbe—as how there's a rope stretched acrost all Moscow.

ANDREY. What for?

FERAPONT. How do I know? The contractor said so.

---

28 The classical dish for Butter Week is pancakes made of raised flour or buckwheat dough, fried in plenty of butter and filled with cottage cheese. The round shape was to represent the sun, since this was originally a pagan holiday.

ANDREY. Don't be silly. (*Reads the book.*) Were you ever in Moscow?

FERAPONT (*after a pause*). I was not. 'Tweren't God's will.

Pause.

Can I go?

ANDREY. You may go. Keep well.

FERAPONT exits.

Keep well. (*Reading.*) Come back tomorrow morning, pick up the paper . . . Go on . . .

Pause.

He's gone. (*The doorbell rings.*) Yes, business . . . (*Stretches and unhurriedly goes back into his room.*)

Offstage a nursemaid is singing a lullaby to a baby.
Enter MASHA and VERSHININ. Later, during their
dialogue, the PARLOR MAID lights a lamp
and candles.

MASHA. I don't know. (*Pause.*) I don't know. Of course, habit has a lot to do with it. After Father died, for instance, it was a long time before we could get used to not having orderlies anymore. But, habit aside, I think I'm being impartial. Maybe it isn't like this in other places, but in our town the most decent, most honorable and cultured people are the military.

VERSHININ. I'd like something to drink. I could use some tea.

MASHA (*after a glance at the clock*). They'll bring some soon. They married me off when I was eighteen, and I was afraid of my husband because he was a schoolteacher and at the time I'd just graduated. At the time he seemed to me to be terribly clever, learned, and important. But that's no longer the case, sad to say.

VERSHININ. Is that so . . . yes.

MASHA. I'm not including my husband, I'm used to him, but among civilians in general there so many crude, uncongenial, uncouth people. I get upset, I'm offended by crudeness, it pains me to see a man who's not as refined or sensitive or congenial as he should be. When I have to be with schoolteachers, my husband's colleagues, I'm just in agony.

VERSHININ. Yes, ma'am . . . But I don't think it matters much, civilian or military, they're equally uninteresting, at least in this town. Makes no difference! If you listen to any educated man in this town, civilian or military, he's sick and tired of his wife, sick and tired of his home, sick and tired of his estate, sick and tired of his horses . . . A Russian is highly capable of coming up with advanced ideas, so tell me, why is his aim in life so low? Why?

MASHA. Why?

VERSHININ. Why is he sick and tired of his children, sick and tired of his wife? And why are his wife and children sick and tired of him?

MASHA. You're in a bad mood today.

VERSHININ. Could be. I haven't had dinner today, I've eaten nothing since this morning. One of my daughters is under the weather, and when my little girls are ill, anxiety gets the better of me. My conscience bothers me for giving them such a mother. Oh, if only you could have seen her today! So petty! We started bickering at seven in the morning, and at nine I slammed the door and went out.

Pause.

I never talk about this, and it's strange, you're the only one I complain to. (*Kisses her hand.*) Don't be angry with me. Except for you, only you, I have no one, no one . . .

Pause.

MASHA. What a racket in the stove! Not long before Father died, there was a whistling in our stovepipe. It was exactly like that.

VERSHININ. You're superstitious?

MASHA. Yes.

VERSHININ. 'S funny. (*Kisses her hand.*) You're a superb, a marvelous woman. Superb, marvelous woman! It's dark in here, but I can see the sparkle in your eyes.

MASHA (*moves to another chair*). There's more light over here . . .

VERSHININ. I love, love, love . . . I love your eyes, your movements, which come to me in my dreams . . . Superb, marvelous woman!

MASHA (*laughing quietly*). When you talk to me that way, for some reason I have to laugh, even though I feel terrified. Don't say it again, please don't . . . (*In an undertone.*) Go on, do talk, it doesn't matter to me . . . (*Hides her face in her hands.*) To me it doesn't matter. Someone's coming in here, talk about something else . . .

> *IRINA and TUSENBACH enter through the*
> *reception room.*

TUSENBACH. I have a tripartite name. I'm called Baron Tusenbach-Krone-Altschauer, but I'm a Russian, of the Orthodox faith, same as you. There's only a bit of German left in me, actually only the dogged obstinacy I pester you with. I escort you home every single night.

IRINA. I'm so tired!

TUSENBACH. And every single night I'll come to the telegraph office and escort you home, I will for ten, twenty years, until you chase me away . . . (*On seeing Masha and Vershinin, glee-fully.*) Is that you? Good evening.

IRINA. Here I am, home at last. (*To Masha.*) Just now a lady comes in, wires her brother in Saratov[29] to say that her son has died, and she couldn't manage to remember the address. So she sent it without an address, simply to Saratov. Crying the whole time. And I was rude to her for no reason at all. "I haven't

---

29 A city on the Volga.

got the time," I said. It sounded so stupid. Are the masqueraders dropping by tonight?

MASHA. Yes.

IRINA (*sits in an armchair*). Have to rest. I'm tired.

TUSENBACH (*with a smile*). Whenever you come home from
work, you look so small, such a tiny little thing . . .

Pause.

IRINA. I'm tired. No, I don't like the telegraph office, I don't
like it.

MASHA. You're getting thinner . . . (*Whistles under her breath.*)
And younger, for your face looks just like a sweet little boy's.

TUSENBACH. It's the way she does her hair.

IRINA. I've got to look for another job, this one's not for me. What
I so wanted, what I dream of is definitely missing in this one.
Drudgery without poetry, without thought . . . (*A knock on the
floor.*) The doctor's knocking. (*To Tusenbach.*) Knock back,
my dear. I can't . . . I'm tired . . . (*TUSENBACH knocks on the
floor.*) He'll be here in a minute. Somebody ought to do something about him. Yesterday the Doctor and Andrey were at the
club and lost again. They say Andrey lost two hundred rubles.

MASHA (*indifferently*). What can you do now!

IRINA. Two weeks ago he lost, back in December he lost. If only
he'd hurry up and lose everything, maybe we'd leave this town.
Honest to God, I dream of Moscow every night, I'm getting

to be a regular obsessive. (*Laughs.*) We'll move there in June, and till June there's still . . . February, March, April, May . . . almost half a year!

MASHA. Just so long as Natasha hasn't found out about his losses.

IRINA. I shouldn't think it matters to her.

> CHEBUTYKIN, *only just got out of bed—he was
> napping after dinner—enters the reception room and
> combs out his beard, then sits there at the table and
> pulls a newspaper out of his pocket.*

MASHA. Here he comes . . . Has he paid his room rent?

IRINA (*laughs*). No. For eight months not the slightest kopek. Apparently he's forgotten.

MASHA (*laughs*). How pompously he sits!

> *They all laugh; pause.*

IRINA. Why are you so silent, Colonel?

VERSHININ. I don't know. I'd like some tea. Half my kingdom for a glass of tea![30] I haven't had anything to eat since this morning . . .

CHEBUTYKIN. Irina Sergeevna!

IRINA. What do you want?

---

30 Paraphrase of the famous line from Shakespeare's *Richard III*: "A horse! A horse! My kingdom for a horse!" (Act V, scene 4).

CHEBUTYKIN. Please come over here. *Venez ici!*[31] (*IRINA goes and sits at the table.*) I can't live without you. (*IRINA lays out a game of solitaire.*)

VERSHININ. What do you say? If there's no tea, let's at least philosophize.

TUSENBACH. Let's. What about?

VERSHININ. What about? Let's dream a little . . . for instance, about the life to come after us, some two hundred or three hundred years from now.

TUSENBACH. How about this? The people who come after us will fly in hot-air balloons, suit jackets will be cut in a different style, maybe they'll discover a sixth sense and put it to use, but life will stay just the same, life will be hard, full of mysteries, and happy. And a thousand years from now men will sigh in just the same way: "Ah, life is a burden!"—and just as they do now, they'll be scared and resist having to die.

VERSHININ (*after giving it some thought*). How I can put this? I have the impression that everything on earth should be changing little by little and is already changing before our very eyes. In two hundred, three hundred, all right, a thousand years— the time span's of no importance—a new and happy life will come into being. This life is something we won't take part in, of course, but we're living for it now, we work, oh, and we suffer, we are creating it—and this is the one and only purpose of our existence and, if you like, our happiness.

---

31 French: Come here.

MASHA laughs quietly.

TUSENBACH. What's come over you?

MASHA. I don't know. All day long I've been laughing, ever since this morning.

VERSHININ. I finished school at the same grade you did, I didn't go to the Military Academy; I read a great deal, but I don't know how to choose books and maybe I don't read what I should, and yet the more I live, the more I want to know. My hair's turning gray, any day now I'll be an old man, but I know so little, ah, so little! But even so, I think what's most important, what really matters I do know, and know it through and through. If only I could prove to you that there is no happiness, there shouldn't be and will not be for any of us . . . All we should do is work and go on working, as for happiness, that's the lot of future generations.

Pause.

Not my lot but that of future generations of future generations.

FEDOTIK and RODÉ appear in the reception room;
they sit down and sing quietly, strumming on
the guitar.

TUSENBACH. To your way of thinking, a person's not supposed to dream of happiness! But what if I am happy!

VERSHININ. No.

TUSENBACH (*clasping his hands together and laughing*). Obviously, we're not communicating. Well, how can I convince you? (*MASHA laughs quietly.*) (*Wagging a finger at her.*) Go ahead and laugh! (*To Vershinin.*) Not just two hundred or three hundred, but even a million years from now, life will be the same as it's always been; it won't change, it will stay constant, governed by its own laws, which are none of our business or, at least, which we'll never figure out. Birds of passage, cranes, for instance, fly on and on, and whatever thoughts, sublime or trivial, may drift through their heads, they'll keep on flying and never know what for or where to. They fly and will keep on flying, whatever philosopher they may hatch; and let them philosophize to their heart's content, so long as they keep on flying . . .

MASHA. Then what's the point?

TUSENBACH. The point . . . Look, there's snow falling. What's the point of that?

Pause.

MASHA. It seems to me, a person ought to believe in something or look for something to believe in; otherwise his life is empty, empty . . . To live and not know why cranes fly, why children are born, why stars are in the sky . . . Either you know why you live or else it's all senseless, gobbledy-gook.

Pause.

VERSHININ. Still it's a pity that youth has flown . . .

MASHA. In one of Gogol's stories, he says: It's a sad world, my masters![32]

TUSENBACH. And I say: it's hard to argue with you, my masters! You're too much . . .

CHEBUTYKIN (*reading the paper*). Balzac was married in Berdichev.[33] (*IRINA sings quietly.*) That's something to jot down in the book. (*Jots it down.*) Balzac was married in Berdichev. (*Reads the paper.*)

IRINA (*laying out a game of solitaire; pensively*). Balzac was married in Berdichev.

TUSENBACH. The die is cast.[34] You know, Mariya Sergeevna, I've turned in my resignation.

MASHA. So I've heard. And I doubt anything good will come of it. I don't like civilians.

TUSENBACH. Doesn't matter . . . (*Rises.*) I'm not good-looking, what kind of military figure do I cut? Besides, it doesn't matter, anyway . . . I'll go to work. At least once in my life I'll do some work, so I can come home at night, collapse on my bed

---

32 Masha is quoting the last sentence of Gogol's "Story of How Ivan Ivanovich and Ivan Nikiforovich Fell Out" (1832): literally, "It's boring in this world, gentlemen." Like Gogol's heroes, Tusenbach and Vershinin will never agree.

33 The French novelist Honoré de Balzac (1799–1850) married the Polish landowner Ewelyna Hanska in Berdichev a few months before he died. Berdichev, a city in the Kiev *guberniya* in Ukraine, was almost entirely populated by Jews, hence the incongruity.

34 Spoken by Julius Caesar on crossing the Rubicon, as related in Suetonius, *Lives of the Twelve Caesars.*

exhausted and fall fast asleep in an instant. (*Going into the reception room.*) I suppose workingmen sleep soundly!

FEDOTIK (*to Irina*). Just now at Pyzhikov's on Moscow Street I bought you some colored pencils. And here's a little penknife.

IRINA. You're used to treating me like a child, but I really am grown up now . . . (*Takes the pencils and penknife; with delight.*) What fun!

FEDOTIK. And for myself I bought a jackknife . . . here, have a look at it . . . one blade, then another blade, a third, that's for cleaning out the ears, this is a tiny scissors, this one's for trimming nails . . .

RODÉ (*loudly*). Doctor, how old are you?

CHEBUTYKIN. Me? Thirty-two.

Laughter.

FEDOTIK. Now I'm going to show you another kind of solitaire . . . (*Deals out a game of solitaire.*)

The samovar is brought in. ANFISA is by the samovar;
a bit of a wait and then NATASHA enters and also
fusses around the samovar. SOLYONY enters and,
after exchanging greetings, sits at the table.

VERSHININ. Incidentally, that's quite a wind!

MASHA. Yes. I'm sick and tired of winter. I've already forgot what summer's like.

IRINA. The solitaire's coming out, I see. We'll be in Moscow.

FEDOTIK. No it isn't. You see, the eight was on top of the deuce of spades. (*Laughs.*) That means, you won't be in Moscow.

CHEBUTYKIN (*reads the paper*). Tsitsikar.[35] Smallpox is raging there.

ANFISA (*coming over to Masha*). Masha, have some tea, dearie. (*To Vershinin.*) Please, your honor . . . forgive me, dearie, I've forgot your name . . .

MASHA. Bring it here, Nanny. I refuse to go in there.

IRINA. Nanny!

ANFISA. Co-oming!

NATASHA (*to Solyony*). Breastfed children understand one perfectly. "Good morning," I'll say, "Good morning, Bobik darling!" He'll stare at me in a special sort of way. You probably think that's the mother in me talking but no, no, absolutely not! He's an exceptional baby.

SOLYONY. If that baby were mine, I'd fry him in a pan and eat him. (*Takes his glass into the drawing-room and sits in a corner.*)

NATASHA (*hiding her face in her hands*). Rude, uncouth man!

MASHA. Happy the man who doesn't notice whether it's summer or winter. I think if I were in Moscow, I wouldn't pay any attention to the weather . . .

---

35 Or Tsitisar or Qiqihar or Ho-lung-kiang, a province of Chinese Manchuria.

VERSHININ. A few days ago I was reading the diary of a French cabinet minister, written in prison. The cabinet minister had been sentenced for taking bribes in the Panama scandal.[36] With what intoxication, what ecstasy he recalls the birds he saw from his prison window and which he failed to notice before when he was a cabinet minister. Of course, now that he's released and at liberty, he's stopped noticing birds, just as before. And you'll stop noticing Moscow once you're living there. We have no happiness, there is none, we only long for it.

TUSENBACH (*takes a little box from the table*). Where are the chocolates?

IRINA. Solyony ate them.

TUSENBACH. All of 'em?

ANFISA (*handing round the tea*). There's a letter for you, dearie.

VERSHININ. For me? (*Takes the letter.*) From my daughters. (*Reads.*) Yes, naturally . . . Excuse me, Mariya Sergeevna, I'll leave ever so quietly. I won't have any tea. (*Rises in great agitation.*) These everlasting scenes . . .

MASHA. What is it? Not a secret?

---

36 *Impressions cellulaires*, by Charles Baïhaut (1834–1905), French Minister for Panama, who was condemned to two years in prison in 1893. Chekhov had read this book during his stay in Nice in 1897. The bankruptcy in 1888 of the company organized to build the Panama canal resulted in the conviction of several French politicians for fraud.

VERSHININ (*quietly*). My wife poisoned herself again. I've got to go. I'll slip out without being noticed. Awfully unpleasant all this. (*Kisses Masha's hand.*) My dear, wonderful, lovely woman . . . I'll slip out of here ever so quietly . . . (*Exits.*)

ANFISA. Where's he off to? Why, I gave him tea . . . What a one.

MASHA (*losing her temper*). Stop it! Forever badgering us, you never give us a moment's peace . . . (*Goes with her cup to the table.*) I'm sick and tired of you, old woman!

ANFISA. Why are you so touchy? Sweetheart!

ANDREY'S VOICE. Anfisa!

ANFISA (*mimics*). Anfisa! There he sits . . . (*Exits.*)

MASHA (*in the reception room at the table, angrily*). Do let me sit down! (*Messes up the cards on the table.*) Sprawling all over with your cards. Drink your tea!

IRINA. Mashka, you're being nasty.

MASHA. If I'm nasty, don't talk to me. Don't touch me!

CHEBUTYKIN (*laughing*). Don't touch her, don't touch . . .

MASHA. You're sixty years old, but you're like a snotty little boy, nobody knows what the hell you're babbling about.

NATASHA (*sighs*). Masha dear, what's the point of using such expressions in polite conversation? With your lovely looks you'd be simply enchanting in decent society, I'll say that straight to your face, if it weren't for that vocabulary of yours. *Je vous prie, pardonnez moi, Marie, mais vous avez des manières un peu grossières.*[37]

TUSENBACH (*restraining his laughter*). May I . . . may I . . . I think there's some cognac . . .

NATASHA. *Il paraît, que mon Bobik déjà ne dort pas,*[38] he woke up. He isn't well today. I'll go to him, excuse me . . . (*Exits.*)

IRINA. But where has the Colonel gone?

MASHA. Home. His wife again—something unexpected.

TUSENBACH (*goes to Solyony, carrying a decanter of cognac*). You always sit by yourself, thinking about something—and you have no idea what. Well, let's make peace. Let's have some cognac. (*They drink.*) I'll have to tickle the ivories all night tonight, I suppose, play all sorts of trash . . . Come what may!

SOLYONY. Why make peace? I haven't quarreled with you.

TUSENBACH. You always make me feel that something has happened between us. You've got a strange personality, you must admit.

---

37 French: Please, forgive me, Marie, but you have rather rude manners. French was common in Russian intellectual circles, but it is pretentious on the part of Natasha, who makes frequent mistakes. Correctly, it would be *"je vous en prie."*

38 Bad French: It seems my Bobik is already not asleep.

SOLYONY (*declaiming*). "Strange I may be, but then who is not?"[39] "Contain your wrath, Aleko!"[40]

TUSENBACH. What's Aleko got to do with it . . .

Pause.

SOLYONY. When I'm alone with anyone, it's all right, I'm like everybody else, but in company I'm dejected, inhibited, and . . . I talk all sorts of rubbish. But all the same I'm more honest and decent than lots and lots of people. And I can prove it.

TUSENBACH. I often get angry with you, you're constantly needling me when we're in public, but all the same for some reason I have an affinity to you. Come what may, I'll get drunk tonight. Let's drink!

SOLYONY. Let's drink. (*They drink.*) I don't have anything against you, Baron. But my temperament is like Lermontov's. (*Quietly.*) I even look a little like Lermontov[41] . . . so they

---

39 Quotation from the classic comedy *Woe from Wit* by Aleksandr Griboedov, a line of the protagonist Chatsky (Act V, scene 1), who is in opposition to Moscow's high society and its blind Francophilia.

40 Aleko is the hero of the romantic verse tale "The Gypsies," by Aleksandr Pushkin (1824), heavily influenced by Byronic romanticism. A Russian depressed by civilization, Aleko turns his back on elegant Petersburg and lives with gypsies; he falls in love with a gypsy girl and commits a murder out of jealousy. Rachmaninov turned it into an opera (1892).

41 Mikhail Yuryevich Lermontov (1814–1841), after Pushkin the most important lyric poet of Russian Romanticism. As an officer, Lermontov was twice exiled to the Caucasus, then killed in a duel. "Actually, Solyony does think that he looks like Lermontov, but of course he doesn't—it's ridiculous just to think of . . . He should be made up to look like Lermontov. The resemblance to Lermontov is enormous, but only in Solyony's mind" (Chekhov to I. A. Tikhomirov, January 14, 1901).

say . . . (*Takes the flask of perfume from his pocket and sprinkles it on his hands.*)

TUSENBACH. I've turned in my resignation. *Basta!* For five years I kept turning it over in my mind and finally I came to a decision. I shall go to work.

SOLYONY (*declaiming*). "Contain your wrath, Aleko . . . Forget, forget your dreams . . ."

> *While they talk, ANDREY enters with a book and sits by the candles.*

TUSENBACH. I shall go to work.

CHEBUTYKIN (*going into the drawing-room with IRINA*). And the refreshments were also authentic Caucasian dishes: onion soup and for the roast—chekhartma, a meat dish.

SOLYONY. Cheremsha[42] isn't meat at all, but a vegetable related to our onion.

CHEBUTYKIN. No sir, angel mine. Chekhartma is not an onion, but roast mutton.

SOLYONY. And I tell you, cheremsha is onion.

CHEBUTYKIN. And I tell you, chekhartma is mutton.

SOLYONY. And I tell you, cheremsha is onion.

---

42 *Chekhartma*, correctly, *chikhartma*, is a Caucasian soup of lamb or chicken, flavored with coriander and saffron. *Cheremsha* may refer to either *cheremitsa* (masculine, *Allium angulosum*), the sharp-edged leek, or *cheremitsa* (feminine, *Allium ursinum*), wild garlic.

CHEBUTYKIN. Why should I argue with you? You were never in the Caucasus and never ate chekhartma.

SOLYONY. I never ate it, because I can't stand it. Cheremsha reeks as badly as garlic.

ANDREY (*pleading*). That's enough, gentlemen! For pity's sake!

TUSENBACH. When do the masqueraders get here?

IRINA. They promised to be here by nine, which means any minute now.

TUSENBACH (*embraces Andrey*). "Ah, you gates, my gates, new gates . . ."

ANDREY (*dances and sings*). "New gates, made of maple . . ."

CHEBUTYKIN (*dances*). "Lattice-grates upon my gates!"[43]

Laughter.

TUSENBACH (*kisses Andrey*). Damn it, let's have a drink. Andryusha, let's drink to being old pals. And I'm going with you, Andryusha, to Moscow, to the university.

SOLYONY. Which one? In Moscow there are two universities.

ANDREY. In Moscow there is one university.

SOLYONY. And I tell you—two.

ANDREY. Make it three. The more the merrier.

---

43 A folk song sung as accompaniment to vigorous dancing.

SOLYONY. In Moscow there are two universities! (*Grumbling and hissing.*) In Moscow there are two universities: the old one and the new one. And if you don't enjoy listening to me, if my words annoy you, then I can stop talking. I can even go off into another room . . . (*Exits through one of the doors.*)

TUSENBACH. Bravo, bravo! (*Laughs.*) Gentlemen, proceed, I shall commence to play! Laughable that Solyony . . . (*Sits down at the baby grand, plays a waltz.*)

MASHA (*dances a waltz by herself*). Baron's drunk, Baron's drunk, Baron's drunk!

Enter NATASHA.

NATASHA (*to Chebutykin*). Ivan Romanych! (*Mentions something to Chebutykin, then quietly exits.*)

CHEBUTYKIN taps Tusenbach on the shoulder and whispers something to him.

IRINA. What is it?

CHEBUTYKIN. Time for us to go. Be well.

TUSENBACH. Good night. Time to go.

IRINA. Excuse me . . . But what about the masqueraders? . . .

ANDREY (*embarrassed*). There won't be any masqueraders. You see, my dear, Natasha says that Bobik isn't very well, and so . . . To make a long story short, I don't know anything about it, it doesn't matter to me in the least.

IRINA (*shrugging*). Bobik isn't well!

MASHA. Now we've had it! They're kicking us out, so I suppose we've got to go. (*To Irina.*) It's not Bobik that's sick, it's her . . . Here! (*Taps her forehead with a finger.*) Small-town slut![44]

> ANDREY *exits through the door right, to his room,*
> CHEBUTYKIN *follows him; those in the reception*
> *room say good-bye.*

FEDOTIK. What a shame! I'd counted on spending a full night here, but if the little baby's ill, then, of course . . . Tomorrow I'll bring him a little toy . . .

RODÉ (*loudly*). I deliberately took a nap after dinner today, I thought I'd be up all night dancing. After all, it's only nine o'clock now!

MASHA. Let's go out in the street and discuss it there. We'll come up with something to do.

> *"Good-bye! Keep well!" can be heard, as well as the*
> *merry laughter of TUSENBACH. ANFISA and*
> *the PARLOR MAID clear the table and extinguish*
> *the lights. The nursemaid can be heard singing.*
> *Enter quietly ANDREY in an overcoat and hat and*
> CHEBUTYKIN.

CHEBUTYKIN. I didn't have a chance to get married, because life flashed by me like a streak of lightning, and besides I was madly in love with your dear mother, who was married already . . .

---

44 *Meshchanka*, literally, petty-bourgeois female, commoner. Natasha is a social inferior to the Prozorovs, who come from the gentry.

ANDREY. There's no reason to get married. No reason, because it's a bore.

CHEBUTYKIN. That may be so, but then there's the loneliness. However much you philosophize, loneliness is a terrible thing, my boy . . . Although, basically . . . Of course, it doesn't matter!

ANDREY. Let's go quickly.

CHEBUTYKIN. What's the rush? We've got time.

ANDREY. I'm afraid the wife might stop me.

CHEBUTYKIN. Ah!

ANDREY. I won't play tonight, I'll just sit and watch. I don't feel well . . . Doctor, what should I take for shortness of breath?

CHEBUTYKIN. Why ask! I don't remember, my boy. I don't know.

ANDREY. Let's go through the kitchen.

They leave.

The doorbell rings, then rings again: voices and laughter are heard.

IRINA (*enters*). What's that?

ANFISA (*in a whisper*). Masqueraders!

The doorbell.

IRINA. Nanny dear, say no one's at home. Make excuses.

[127]

*ANFISA exits. IRINA walks about the room in a
revery; she is on edge. Enter SOLYONY.*

SOLYONY (*bewildered*). No one's here . . . But where are they all?

IRINA. They went home.

SOLYONY. Strange. You're alone here?

IRINA. Alone. (*Pause.*) Good-bye.

SOLYONY. A while ago I behaved without proper restraint and discretion. But you aren't like the rest, you're exalted and pure, you can discern the truth . . . You alone, only you can understand me. I love, I love profoundly, incessantly . . .

IRINA. Good-bye! Go away.

SOLYONY. I can't live without you. (*Following her around.*) Oh, my heaven on earth! (*Plaintively.*) Oh, happiness! exquisite, wonderful, bewitching eyes, I've never seen their like in any other woman . . .

IRINA (*coldly*). Stop it, Vasily Vasilich!

SOLYONY. This is the first time I'm talking to you of love, and it's exactly like being out of this world, on another planet. (*Rubs his forehead.*) Well, still, it doesn't matter. You can't be compelled to care for me, of course . . . But I won't tolerate any successful rivals . . . Won't tolerate it . . . I swear to you by all that's holy, I'll kill any rival . . . Oh, wonderful woman!

NATASHA passes through with a candle.

NATASHA (*peers through one door, then another, and passes the door leading to her husband's room*). Andrey's in there. Let him read. Do forgive me, Vasily Vasilich, I didn't know you were here, I'm in a housecoat.

SOLYONY. It doesn't matter to me. Good-bye! (*Exits.*)

NATASHA. And you're tired, darling, my poor little girl. (*Kisses Irina.*) You should have gone to bed much sooner.

IRINA. Is Bobik asleep?

NATASHA. He's asleep. But he sleeps so restlessly. By the way, darling, I wanted to tell you, but you're never around, or I never have the time . . . Bobik's present nursery seems to me to be cold and damp. But your room is so right for a baby. Dearest, sweetheart, move in with Olya for a while!

IRINA (*confused*). Where?

A troika with harness bells can be heard pulling up to the house.

NATASHA. You and Olya can be in one room for a while, and your room will go to Bobik. He's such a little darling, today I say to him, "Bobik, you're mine! All mine!" And he stares at me with his pretty little peepers. (*Doorbell.*) That's Olga, I suppose. Isn't she late! (*The PARLOR MAID walks over to Natasha and whispers in her ear.*) Protopopov? What a character. Protopopov's here and wants me to go for a ride with him in the troika.[45] (*Laughs.*) How funny men are . . . (*Doorbell.*) Someone's ringing . . . Olga's back, I suppose. (*Exits.*)

The PARLOR MAID runs out; IRINA sits rapt in thought; enter KULYGIN and OLGA, followed by VERSHININ.

KULYGIN. Would you look at this. But they said they'd be having a party.

VERSHININ. Strange, I left not long ago, half an hour, and they were waiting for the masqueraders . . .

IRINA. They've all gone.

KULYGIN. Masha's gone too? Where did she go? And why is Protopopov downstairs waiting in a troika? Who's he waiting for?

IRINA. Don't give me a quiz . . . I'm tired.

KULYGIN. Temper, temper . . .

OLGA. The meeting only just ended. I'm exhausted. Our headmistress is ill, and I'm taking her place now. My head, my head aches, my head . . . (*Sits.*) Andrey lost two hundred rubles at cards yesterday . . . The whole town's talking about it.

KULYGIN. Yes, the meeting wore me out too. (*Sits.*)

VERSHININ. My wife just now took it into her head to give me a scare, she all but poisoned herself. It's all blown over, and

---

45 Sleigh rides, preferably in a troika, decorated with colored ribbons and bells, were a favorite pastime during *Maslennitsa*. The sleighs would travel in wide semicircles to commemorate the sun's passage.

I'm relieved, I can take it easy now . . . So, I suppose, we've got to go? Well then, let me wish you all the best. Fyodor Ilyich, walk somewhere with me! I can't stay at home, I simply cannot . . . Let's go for a walk!

KULYGIN. I'm tired. I'm going nowhere. (*Rises.*) I'm tired. Did my wife go home?

IRINA. I suppose so.

KULYGIN (*kisses Irina's hand*). Good-bye. Tomorrow and the day after I've got the whole day to relax. All the best! (*Goes.*) I'd really like some tea. I counted on spending the evening in congenial company and—*o, fallacem hominum spem!*[46] . . . Accusative case, used in the vocative . . .

VERSHININ. Which means, I'm on my own. (*Exits with KULY-GIN, whistling.*)

OLGA. My head aches, my poor head . . . Andrey lost . . . the whole town's talking . . . I'll go lie down. (*Goes.*) Tomorrow I'm free . . . Oh, goodness, how nice it'll be! Free tomorrow, free the day after . . . My head aches, my poor head . . . (*Exits.*)

IRINA (*alone*). They've all gone. No one's left.

In the street there's a concertina, the NURSEMAID
sings a song.

---

46 Latin: "oh, vain is human hope!" from Cicero, *The Orator* (III, ii).

NATASHA (*wearing a fur coat and hat walks through the reception room, followed by the PARLOR MAID*). I'll be back in half an hour. Just going for a little ride. (*Exits.*)

IRINA (*alone, yearning*). To Moscow! To Moscow! To Moscow!

Curtain

ACT THREE

Olga's and Irina's room. Beds at left and right, fenced round with screens. Between two and three o'clock in the morning. Offstage an alarm bell is ringing to fight a fire that started much earlier. Quite clearly no one in the house has been to bed yet. On a sofa lies MASHA, dressed, as usual, in black.

Enter OLGA and ANFISA.

ANFISA. They're sitting downstairs now under the staircase . . . And I says, "Please go upstairs," I says, "'tain't right for you to sit here,"—they're crying. "Papa," they says, "we don't know where he's at. God forbid," they says, "he ain't burnt up." Where they'd get a notion like that! And there's some more in the yard . . . undressed too.

OLGA (*pulls dresses out of a wardrobe*). Here, take this gray one . . . And this one too . . . The housecoat as well . . . And take this skirt, my dear . . . What a thing to happen, dear God! Kirsanov Lane is burnt to the ground, it seems. (*Flings the dresses into her arms.*) The poor Vershinins are in a panic . . . Their house was nearly burned down. Have them spend the night with us . . . we can't let them go home . . . At poor Fedotik's everything was burnt, nothing was saved . . .

ANFISA. You'd better call Ferapont, Olyushka, otherwise I can't handle it all . . .

OLGA (*rings*). I'm not getting through . . . (*Out the door.*) Come in here, somebody!

> *Through the open door can be seen a window, red with the glow in the sky, and the fire brigade can be heard driving past the house.*

How horrible. And I'm sick and tired of it!

> *Enter FERAPONT.*

Here, take this and carry it downstairs . . . The young Kolotilin ladies are standing under the stairs . . . give it to them. And give them this . . .

FERAPONT. Yes, ma'am. In the year '12 Moscow was burned down too. Lord God almighty! It sure surprised the Frenchies.[47]

OLGA. Go, go on . . .

FERAPONT. Yes ma'am. (*Exits.*)

---

47 Ferapont alludes to the burning of Moscow in 1812 during its occupation by Napoleon's troops. No one knows for sure, but rumor had it that the Russians started the fire.

OLGA. Nanny dear, darling, give it all away. We don't need any of it, give it all away, nanny dear . . . I'm worn out, can barely stand on my feet . . . we can't let the Vershinins go home . . . The little girls will sleep in the drawing-room, have the Colonel go to the baron's . . . Fedotik can go to the baron's too, or let him stay here with us in the reception room . . . The Doctor, as if he did it on purpose, is drunk, hideously drunk, and no one can be put in with him. And Vershinin's wife in the drawing-room too.

ANFISA (*faintly*). Olyushka darling, don't drive me away! Don't drive me away!

OLGA. Don't be silly, Nanny. No one's going to drive you away.

ANFISA (*lays her head on Olga's bosom*). My love, my precious, I toil, I work . . . I'm getting feeble, everybody says, get out! And where am I to go? Where? In my eighties. My eighty-second year . . .

OLGA. You sit down, Nanny dear . . . You're tired, poor thing . . . (*Helps her sit down.*) Have a rest, my dear. How pale she is!

NATASHA enters.

NATASHA. Downstairs they're saying somebody ought to hurry and organize a committee in aid of the fire victims. Why not? It's a lovely idea. As a rule one ought to help the poor, it's an obligation of the rich. Bobik and Sophiekins are asleep, asleep as if nothing had happened. We've got so many people all over the place, wherever you go, the house is packed. There's flu going around town now, I'm worried the children might catch it.

OLGA (*not listening to her*). You can't see the fire from this room, it's peaceful here . . .

. **NATASHA.** Yes . . . I suppose I look a mess. (*Before a mirror.*) They say I'm putting on weight . . . it's not true! Not a bit of it! And Masha's asleep, worn out, poor thing . . . (*To Anfisa, coldly.*) Don't you dare sit in my presence! Stand up! Get out of here! (*ANFISA exits; pause.*) And why you hold on to that old woman I cannot understand!

OLGA (*startled*). Excuse me, I can't understand either . . .

NATASHA. There's no reason for her to be here. She's a peasant, ought to live in the country . . . It's pampering them! I like a house to be in order! There shouldn't be any useless people in a house. (*Stroking Olga's cheek.*) You're tired, poor dear! Our headmistress is tired! Why, when my Sophiekins is a big girl and goes to high school, I'll be afraid of you.

OLGA. I'm not going to be headmistress.

NATASHA. They'll pick you, Olga sweetie. The decision's made.

OLGA. I'll turn it down. I cannot . . . I haven't the strength for it . . . (*Drinks some water.*) Just now you abused Nanny so rudely . . . Forgive me, I'm in no condition to put up with . . . It's going dark before my eyes . . .

. **NATASHA** (*agitated*). Forgive me, Olya, forgive . . . I didn't mean to upset you.

    MASHA gets up, takes a pillow and exits, angrily.

OLGA. Try to understand, dear . . . Perhaps we've had a strange upbringing, but I cannot tolerate this. That sort of behavior depresses me, it makes me ill . . . My heart just sinks!

NATASHA. Forgive me, forgive me . . . (*Kisses her.*)

OLGA. Any coarseness, even the slightest, an indelicately spoken word upsets me . . .

NATASHA. I often say too much, that's true, but you must agree, my dear, she could live in the country.

OLGA. She's been with us thirty years.

NATASHA. But she's incapable of working now! Either I don't understand you or else you refuse to understand me. She's not fit for housework, she only sleeps or sits.

OLGA. Then let her sit.

NATASHA (*in wonderment*). What do you mean, let her sit? Why, she's a servant, isn't she! (*Plaintively.*) I don't understand you, Olya. I have a nursemaid, I have a wetnurse, I have a parlor maid, a cook . . . what do we need this old woman for? What for?

Offstage the alarm bell is rung.

OLGA. I've aged ten years tonight.

NATASHA. We've got to thrash this out, Olya, once and for all . . . You're at the high school, I'm at home, you have your teaching, I have my housework. And when I put in a word about servants, I know what I'm talking about; I know what I am talking about . . . And so tomorrow will see the last of that thieving old crow, that nasty old hag . . . (*Stamps her foot.*) that witch! . . . Don't you dare provoke me! Don't you dare! (*Recollecting herself.*) Honestly, if you don't move downstairs, why, we'll always be quarreling. It's awful.

Enter KULYGIN.[48]

KULYGIN. Where's Masha? It's high time we went home. They say the fire's dying down. (*Stretching.*) Only one ward was burnt, but the wind was so strong that it looked at first as if the whole town would go up in flames. (*Sits down.*) I'm worn out. Olechka, my dear . . . I often think: if it hadn't been for Masha, I would have married you, Olechka. You're very good . . . I'm exhausted. (*Hearkening to something.*)

OLGA. What?

KULYGIN. To make matters even worse, the doctor's on a bender, he's awfully drunk. To make matters even worse! (*Stands up.*) There, sounds like he's coming in here . . . You hear him? Yes, in here . . . (*Laughs.*) What a one, honestly . . . I'll hide. (*Goes in the corner next to the wardrobe.*) What a delinquent!

OLGA. For two years he hasn't touched a drop, and now all of a sudden he goes and gets drunk . . . (*Goes with NATASHA to the back of the room.*)

---

48 "In Act Three, of course, you can appear in a double-breasted uniform tunic, that's right, but why in Act Two should you come into the drawing-room in a fur coat?" (Chekhov to Aleksandr Vishnevsky, January 17 [30], 1901).

*CHEBUTYKIN enters; not staggering, seemingly
sober, he crosses the room, stops, looks, then walks over
to the washbasin and starts to wash his hands.*

CHEBUTYKIN (*surly*). Damn 'em all to hell . . . ram 'em all . . .[49]
They think I'm a doctor, know how to treat all sorts of ailments,
but I don't know a blessed thing, forgot anything I ever knew,
don't remember a thing, not a blessed thing.

OLGA and NATASHA leave, unnoticed by him.

To hell with 'em. Last Wednesday I treated a woman at
Zasyp—she died, and it's my fault she died. Yes . . . I did
know something twenty-five years ago or so, but now I don't
remember a thing. Not a thing . . . My head's empty, my
soul's frozen. Maybe I'm not even a human being, but just
seem to have arms and legs . . . and a head; maybe I don't
even exist at all, but it just seems to me I walk, eat, sleep.
(*Weeps.*) Oh, if only I didn't exist! (*Stops weeping, surly.*)
Who the hell knows . . . Day before yesterday talk at the club;
they're dropping names, Shakespeare, Voltaire . . . I haven't
read 'em, haven't read 'em at all, but I made a face to show
I'd read 'em. And the others did the same as me. Shabby
and vulgar and vile! And that woman that died on Wednesday, I remembered her . . . and remembered it all, and my
soul turned all twisted, repulsive, foul . . . I went out, started
drinking . . .

---

49 Rhyming wordplay in Russian, "*chyort by pobral . . . podral*" (May the devil carry
you off, may the devil thrash you soundly).

IRINA, VERSHININ, and TUSENBACH enter;
TUSENBACH is wearing civilian clothes, new
and fashionable.

IRINA. Let's sit down here. No one will come in here.

VERSHININ. If it hadn't been for the soldiers, the whole town would have burnt down. Fine lads! (*Rubs his hands in satisfaction.*) Sterling fellows! ah, what fine lads!

KULYGIN (*walking over to them*). What time is it, gentlemen?

TUSENBACH. Four o'clock already. Getting light.

IRINA. Everyone's sitting in the reception room, no one will leave. That Solyony of yours is sitting there too . . . (*To Chebutykin.*) You should be in bed, Doctor.

CHEBUTYKIN. Never mind, ma'am . . . Thank you, ma'am. (*Combs out his beard.*)

KULYGIN (*laughs*). You're sploshified, Doctor! (*Claps him on the shoulder.*) Attaboy! *In vino veritas,*[50] said the ancients.

TUSENBACH. They keep asking me to organize a concert on behalf of the fire victims.

IRINA. Why, who could . . .

TUSENBACH. A person could organize one, if a person wanted to. Your sister Mariya, for instance, plays the piano marvelously.

KULYGIN. Marvelously is the way she plays!

---

50 Latin: in wine lies truth.

IRINA. By now she's forgotten. She hasn't played for three years
. . . or four.

TUSENBACH. Absolutely no one in this town understands music,
not a single soul, but I do understand it and I give you my word of
honor, your sister Mariya plays magnificently, there's talent there.

KULYGIN. You're right, Baron. I love her very much, my Masha.
She's superb.

TUSENBACH. To be able to play so splendidly and at the same
time to realize that no one, absolutely no one understands you!

KULYGIN (*sighs*). Yes . . . But is it proper for her to take part in
a concert? (*Pause.*) Of course I know nothing about it, gentlemen. Perhaps it might even be a good thing. Still, I must confess, our headmaster is a good man, a very good man indeed,
the most intelligent of men, but the views he holds . . . Of
course, it's none of my business, but even so, if you like, I can
probably talk to him about it.

*CHEBUTYKIN picks up a porcelain clock in both
hands and scrutinizes it.*

VERSHININ. I got covered in filth at the fire, must look a sight.
(*Pause.*) Yesterday I heard in passing that they intend to transfer
our brigade somewhere far away. Some say, to the Kingdom of
Poland, others—possibly to Chita.[51]

---

51 Poland at this time was a vice-regency of the Russian Empire. Chita was far away
in the opposite direction, the capital of the region of Transbaikal, Siberia, on the
Chinese frontier.

TUSENBACH. I heard that too. Then what? The town will be quite empty.

IRINA. And we shall go away!

CHEBUTYKIN (*drops the clock, which shatters in pieces*). Smithereens!

Pause; everyone is distressed and embarrassed.

KULYGIN (*picks up the fragments*). To break such an expensive object—ah, Ivan Romanych, Ivan Romanych! You get F minus for conduct![52]

IRINA. That clock was our poor mama's.

CHEBUTYKIN. Could be . . . If it's mama's, then it's mama's. Could be I didn't break it, it only seems like I broke it. Maybe it only seems to us that we exist, but as a matter of fact we don't. I don't know anything, nobody knows anything. (*At the door.*) What are you staring at? Natasha's having a cute little affair with Protopopov, and you don't see it . . . There you sit and don't see a thing, while Natasha's having a little affair with Protopopov . . . (*Sings.*) "A fig for you and tell me how you like it . . ."[53] (*Exits.*)

VERSHININ. Yes . . . (*Laughs.*) How altogether strange this is! When the fire broke out, I rushed home right away; I get there,

---

52 In Russian schools, grades ran from five to one, with five being highest. In Chekhov's original, Kulygin gives Chebutykin "Zero minus."

53 "Chebutykin sings only the words 'A fig for you and tell me how you like it . . .' They're the words from an operetta that was once put on at the Hermitage Theatre. I don't remember the name . . . Chebutykin shouldn't sing any more than that, otherwise his exit will take too long" (Chekhov to I. A. Tikhomirov, January 14, 1901).

take a look—our house is intact and unharmed and out of danger, but my two little girls are standing on the doorstep in nothing but their underwear, their mother's missing, people are milling about, horses running, dogs, and their little girl faces express alarm, panic, entreaty, I don't know what; my heart clenched when I saw those faces. My God, I think, what else will those girls have to live through in the course of a long life! I grab them, run, and keep thinking that thought: what else will they have to live through in this world!

Alarm bell; pause.

I get here, and their mother's here, shouting, throwing a tantrum.

MASHA enters with a pillow and sits on the sofa.

And when my little girls were standing on the doorstep in nothing but their underwear, barefoot, and the street was red with flames, and there was a terrible racket, it occurred to me that things like that used to happen many years ago when there'd be a sudden enemy invasion, looting and burning . . . And yet, what a fundamental difference there is between how things are now and how they were then! And a little more time will go by, say two hundred, three hundred years, and our present life will be regarded in the same way with horror and contempt, everything that exists now will seem awkward and clumsy and very uncomfortable and strange. Oh, for all we know, what a life that's going to be, what a life! (*Laughs.*) Forgive me, I've started philosophizing again. Do let me go on, ladies and gentlemen. I very much want to philosophize, the fit is on me now.

Pause.

Absolutely everyone's asleep. As I was saying: what a life that's going to be! Can you imagine . . . in town now there are only three like you, in generations to come there'll be more, ever more and more, and there'll come a time when everything will change to be your way, people will live your way, and then even you will become obsolete, people will evolve and be superior to you . . . (*Laughs.*) I'm in a funny mood today. I want like hell to live . . . (*Sings.*) "All ages bend the knee to love, its pangs are blessings from above . . ."[54]

MASHA. Trom-tom-tom.

VERSHININ. Trom-tom . . .

MASHA. Tra-ra-ra?

VERSHININ. Tra-ta-ta. (*Laughs.*)[55]

Enter FEDOTIK.

FEDOTIK (*dances*). All burned up, all burned up! Every last thing!

Laughter.

---

54 Vershinin is singing the opening of Gremin's aria in Chaikovsky's opera *Yevgeny Onegin* (1877), from Pushkin's verse novel.

55 "Vershinin pronounces 'trom-tom-tom' in the form of a question, and you in the form of an answer, and this strikes you as such an original joke that you pronounce this 'trom-trom' with a grin . . . She would *utter* 'trom-trom'—and begin to laugh, but not loudly, just barely. You mustn't create the same kind of character as [Yelena in] *Uncle Vanya* at this point, but someone younger and livelier. Remember that you're easily amused, angered" (Chekhov to Olga Knipper, January 20, [February 2], 1901). Knipper had played Yelena at the Moscow Art Theatre in 1900.

IRINA. What's so funny about that? Everything's burnt?

FEDOTIK (*laughs*). Every last thing. Nothing's left. Even the guitar was burnt, and the camera equipment burnt, and all my letters . . . And the notebook I wanted to give you—burnt too.

Enter SOLYONY.

IRINA. No, please, go away, Vasily Vasilich. You can't come in here.

SOLYONY. Why can the Baron, and not me?

VERSHININ. We'd all better leave, in fact. How's the fire?

SOLYONY. They say it's dying down. No, I find this particularly odd, why can the Baron and why can't I? (*Takes out the flask of perfume and sprinkles it about.*)

VERSHININ. Trom-tom-tom.

MASHA. Trom-tom.

VERSHININ (*laughs; to Solyony*). Let's go into the reception room.

SOLYONY. All right, sir, but we're making a note of it. "I'd make my meaning crystal clear, But 'twould upset the geese, I fear . . ."[56] (*Looking at Tusenbach.*) Cheep, cheep, cheep . . .

He exits with VERSHININ and FEDOTIK.

---

56 The moral of Ivan Krylov's fable *The Geese* (1811), in which the barnyard fowl boast of their ancestors, the geese who saved Rome, but have no merits of their own.

IRINA. That Solyony's smoked up the place . . . (*Startled.*) The Baron's asleep! Baron! Baron!

TUSENBACH (*coming to*). I was tired, though . . . The brickworks . . . I'm not raving, as a matter of fact I'll be going to the brickworks soon, I'll start working there . . . There's been some talk about it already. (*To Irina, tenderly.*) You're so pale, beautiful, bewitching . . . I feel as if your pallor brightens the dark atmosphere like a beacon . . . You're sad, you're dissatisfied with life . . . Oh, come away with me, come away to work together!

MASHA. Nikolay Lvovich, get out of here.

TUSENBACH (*laughing*). You're here? I didn't see you. (*Kisses Irina's hand.*) Good-bye, I'll be going . . . I look at you now and call to mind how once, long ago, on your saint's day, you were confident and carefree and talked of the joys of hard work . . . And what a happy life flashed before me then! Where is it? (*Kisses her hand.*) You've got tears in your eyes. Go to bed, it's daylight already . . . here comes the morning . . . If only I might give my life for you!

MASHA. Nikolay Lvovich, go away! Now really, what . . .

TUSENBACH. I'm going . . . (*Exit.*)

MASHA (*lies down*). You asleep, Fyodor?

KULYGIN. Huh?

MASHA. You should go home.

KULYGIN. My dearest Masha, my dearest Masha . . .

IRINA. She's worn out. You should let her rest, Fedya.

KULYGIN. I'll go right away . . . My wife's lovely, splendid . . . I love you, my one and only . . .

MASHA (*angrily*). *Amo, amas, amat, amamus, amatis, amant.*[57]

KULYGIN (*laughs*). No, really, she's marvelous. I've been married to you for seven years, but it feels as if we were wed only yesterday. Word of honor. No, really, you're a marvelous woman. I'm content, I'm content, I'm content!

MASHA. I'm sick and tired, sick and tired, sick and tired . . . (*Rises to speak in a sitting position.*) I just can't get it out of my head . . . it's simply appalling. Stuck in my brain like a spike, I can't keep quiet. I mean about Andrey . . . He's mortgaged this house to the bank, and his wife snatched all the money, but in fact the house belongs not just to him but to the four of us! He ought to know that, if he's a decent human being.

KULYGIN. Why bother, Masha! What's it to you? Andryusha's in debt all around, so leave him alone.

MASHA. It's appalling in any case. (*Lies down.*)

KULYGIN. You and I aren't poor. I work, I'm at the high school, later in the day I give lessons . . . I'm an honest man. A simple man . . . *Omnia mea mecum porto,*[58] as the saying goes.

---

57 Latin: the basic conjugation of the verb *amare*, to love: I love, thou lovest, he, she, or it loves, we love, you love, they love.

58 Latin: "I carry all my goods on my person," Cicero in *Paradoxa.* Expression of a member of the family of the philosopher Bias fleeing their country before the Persians and refusing to take any worldly goods with him (ca. 570 B.C.).

MASHA. It's not that I need the money, but the unfairness of it galls me.

Pause.

Get going, Fyodor.

KULYGIN (*kisses her*). You're tired, rest for just half an hour, while I sit outside and wait. Get some sleep . . . (*Goes.*) I'm content, I'm content, I'm content. (*Exits.*)

IRINA. As a matter of fact, our Andrey's become so shallow, so seedy and old living with that woman! He used to make plans to be a professor, but yesterday he was boasting that he's finally managed to make member of the County Council. He's a Council member, but Protopopov's the chairman . . . The whole town's talking, laughing, and he's the only one who sees and knows nothing . . . Here again, everybody runs off to the fire, but he sits by himself in his room and pays no attention. All he does is play the violin. (*On edge.*) Oh, it's horrible, horrible, horrible! (*Weeps.*) I cannot, cannot stand it anymore! . . . I cannot, I cannot! . . .

OLGA enters and tidies her night table.

(*Sobs loudly.*) Throw me out, throw me out, I can't stand anymore! . . .

OLGA (*alarmed*). What's wrong, what's wrong? Dearest!

IRINA (*sobbing*). Where? Where has it all gone? Where is it? Oh, my God, my God! I've forgotten everything, forgotten . . . It's all tangled up in my mind . . . I can't remember the Italian for window or, uh, ceiling . . . I forget everything, every day I forget, and life goes on and won't ever, ever come back, we'll never get to Moscow . . . I can see that we won't . . .

OLGA. Dearest, dearest . . .

IRINA (*under control*). Oh, I'm unhappy . . . I cannot work, I will not go on working. Enough, enough! I used to be a telegraph operator, now I work for the town council and I hate, despise whatever they give me to do . . . I'm twenty-four already, I've been working for a long time now, and my brain has dried up, I've got skinny and ugly and old, and I've got nothing, nothing, no sort of satisfaction, while time marches on, and I keep feeling that I'm moving away from a genuine, beautiful life, moving ever farther and farther into some kind of abyss. I'm desperate, I'm desperate! And why I'm still alive, why I haven't killed myself before now, I don't understand . . .

OLGA. Don't cry, my little girl, don't cry . . . It pains me.

IRINA. I'm not crying, not crying . . . Enough . . . There, look, I'm not crying anymore. Enough . . . Enough!

OLGA. Dearest, I'm speaking to you as a sister, as a friend; if you want my advice, marry the Baron! (*IRINA weeps quietly.*) After all, you do respect him, think highly of him . . . True, he's not good looking, but he's so decent, so pure . . . After all, people don't marry for love, but just to do their duty. At least that's how I think of it, and I would marry without love. Anyone who came courting, I'd marry him all the same, I mean if he were a decent man. I'd even marry an old man . . .

IRINA. I kept waiting for us to move to Moscow, there my true love would find me, I would dream about him, love him . . . But it's all turned out to be foolishness, nothing but foolishness.

OLGA (*embraces her sister*). My darling, lovely sister, I understand it all; when the Baron resigned from military service and came calling on us in a suit jacket, he looked so homely I even started to cry . . . He asked me, "What are you crying for?" How could I tell him! But if it were God's will that he marry you, I'd be very happy. That would make a change, a complete change.

> NATASHA, *carrying a candle, crosses the stage from the door right to the door left, in silence.*[59]

MASHA (*sits up*). She prowls around as if she was the one who'd set the fire.

OLGA. Don't be silly, Masha. The silliest in our family, that's you. Forgive me, please.

> *Pause.*

MASHA. I want to make a confession, dear sisters. My heart is heavy, I'll confess to you and never again to anyone, ever . . . I'll speak my piece right now. (*Quietly.*) This is my secret, but you ought to know it all . . . I can't keep still . . .(*Pause.*) I love,

---

59 "You write that in Act Three, Natasha, making the rounds of the house at night, puts out the lights and looks under the furniture for burglars. But, it seems to me, it would be better to have her walk across the stage in a straight line, without a glance at anyone or anything, à la Lady Macbeth, with a candle—something a bit tighter and more frightening" (Chekhov to Olga Knipper, January 2 [15], 1901).

love . . . I love that man . . . You just saw him . . . Well, there you have it. In short, I love Vershinin.[60]

OLGA (*goes behind her screen*). Stop it. It doesn't matter, I'm not listening.

MASHA. What can I do? (*Clutches her head.*) At first he struck me as peculiar, then I felt sorry for him . . . then I fell in love . . .

OLGA (*behind the screen*). I'm not listening, it doesn't matter. Whatever silly things you say, it doesn't matter, I'm not listening.

MASHA. Ay, you're incredible, Olya. I love—which means, it's my fate. Which means, such is my lot . . . And he loves me . . . it's all terrible. Right? it's no good, is it? (*Takes Irina by the hands and draws her to her.*) Oh my dear . . . How are we to get through our lives, what's to become of us . . . When you read a novel, it all seems so trite and so easy to understand, but when you fall in love yourself, you realize that no one knows anything about it and everyone has to decide for herself . . . My dears, my sisters . . . I've confessed to you, now I'll keep still . . . Now I'll be like that madman in Gogol's story . . .[61] still . . . still . . .

Enter ANDREY, followed by FERAPONT.

---

60 "Masha's confession in Act Three is not exactly a confession, but only a frank statement. Behave nervously but not despondently, no shouting, even smiling now and then and for the most part behave so that one can feel the weariness of the night. And so that one can feel that you are more intelligent than your sisters, you think yourself more intelligent, at least. As to 'trom-tom-tom,' do it your way" (Chekhov to Olga Knipper, January 21 [February 3], 1901).

61 Poprishchin, hero of Gogol's story *Diary of a Madman* (1835), is a victim of unrequited love. He continually repeats the phrase "Never mind, never mind . . . be still."

ANDREY (*angrily*). What d'you want? I don't understand.

FERAPONT (*in the doorway, indecisively*). Andrey Sergeich, I already said ten times or so.

ANDREY. In the first place, I'm not Andrey Sergeich to you, I'm Your Honor!

FERAPONT. The firemen, your highness, want to know if you'll let 'em drive across the garden to the river. Otherwise they got to ride round and round in a circle—wears the daylights out of 'em.

ANDREY. All right. Tell them, it's all right. (*FERAPONT exits.*) They make me sick. Where's Olga? (*OLGA appears from behind her screen.*) I came here to get the key to the bookcase, I've lost mine. You've got one of those tiny little keys. (*OLGA gives him the key in silence. IRINA goes behind her screen; pause.*) What a terrific fire, eh! It's starting to die down now. Dammit, that Ferapont got on my nerves, I was talking nonsense . . . Your Honor . . .

> *Pause.*

Why don't you say something, Olga?

> *Pause.*

It's about time you stopped being so silly, pouting like this, acting so high and mighty . . . You're here, Masha, Irina's here, well, that's just fine—let's clear this up right in the open, once and for all. What do you have against me? What?

OLGA. Drop it, Andryusha. We'll clear it up tomorrow. (*Distraught.*) What an excruciating night!

ANDREY (*he's very embarrassed*). Don't get upset. I'm asking this perfectly calmly: what do you have against me? Say it straight out.

VERSHININ's voice: "Trom-tom-tom!"

MASHA (*rises; loudly*). Tra-ta-ta! (*To Olga.*) Good-bye, Olya, God bless you. (*Goes behind the screen, kisses Irina.*) Sleep in peace . . . Good-bye, Andrey. Go away, they're exhausted . . . tomorrow you can clear things up . . . (*Leaves.*)

OLGA. Really, Andryusha, let's put it off till tomorrow . . . (*Goes behind her screen.*) It's time for bed.

ANDREY. I'll just say this and then I'll go. Right away . . . In the first place, you've got something against Natasha, my wife, and I've noticed it from the very day of our wedding. If you want to know, Natasha is a beautiful, honest person, forthright and upstanding—that's my opinion. I love and respect my wife, understand me, respect her and I demand that she be respected by others as well. I repeat, she's an honest, upstanding person, and all your criticism, if you don't mind my saying so, is simply frivolous . . .

Pause.

In the second place, you seem to be angry because I'm not a professor, don't have scholarly pursuits. But I serve the county, I'm a member of the County Council and I consider this service of mine just as dedicated and exalted as service to scholarship. I'm a member of the County Council and proud of it, if you want to know . . .

Pause.

In the third place . . . I've got something else to say . . . I mortgaged the house, without asking your permission . . . There I am at fault, yes, and I beg you to forgive me. I was driven to it by my debts . . . thirty-five thousand . . . I've stopped playing cards, I gave it up a long time ago, but the main thing I can say in my defense is that you're girls, you get Father's pension, but I don't have . . . any income, so to speak . . .

Pause.

KULYGIN (*in the doorway*). Masha's not here? (*Alarmed.*) Where is she? This is odd . . . (*Exits.*)

ANDREY. They aren't listening. Natasha is an excellent, honest person. (*Paces the stage in silence, then stops.*) When I got married, I thought we'd be happy . . . everybody happy . . . But my God . . . (*Weeps.*) My dear sisters, precious sisters, don't believe me, don't believe me . . . (*Exits.*)

KULYGIN (*in the doorway, worried*). Where's Masha? Isn't Masha here then? Amazing. (*Exits.*)

Alarm bell; the stage is empty.

IRINA (*behind a screen*). Olya! Who's that knocking on the floor?

OLGA. It's the Doctor. He's drunk.

IRINA. What a crazy night!

Pause.

Olya! (*Peers out from behind her screen.*) Did you hear? They're taking the brigade away from us, they're transferring it somewhere far away.

OLGA. That's mere rumor.

IRINA. We'll be here all alone then . . . Olya!

OLGA. Well?

IRINA. Dearest, precious, I respect, I think highly of the Baron, he's a fine man, I will marry him, agreed, only let's go to Moscow! Only please, please, let's go! There's nothing on earth better than Moscow! Let's go, Olya! Let's go!

Curtain

ACT FOUR

An old garden attached to the Prozorovs' house. A long path lined with fir trees, at whose end a river can be seen. On the farther bank of the river is a forest. To the right, the veranda of the house; here on a table are bottles and glasses; apparently someone has been drinking champagne. Twelve o'clock noon. Passersby occasionally cut through the garden from the street to the river; five or so soldiers pass quickly by.

CHEBUTYKIN, *in an affable mood that stays with him throughout the whole act, is sitting in an armchair in the garden, waiting to be called; he wears a forage cap and has a walking stick. IRINA, KULYGIN with a medal round his neck and without his moustache, and TUSENBACH, sitting on the veranda, are seeing off FEDOTIK and RODÉ, who are coming down the steps, both officers in field kit.*

TUSENBACH (*exchanging kisses with FEDOTIK*). You're a good man, we were such friends. (*Exchanges kisses with RODÉ.*) One more time . . . Good-bye, my dear friend!

IRINA. See you soon!

FEDOTIK. It isn't see-you-soon, it's good-bye, we'll never meet again!

KULYGIN. Who knows! (*Wipes his eyes, smiles.*) Look, I'm starting to cry.

IRINA. We'll meet some day.

FEDOTIK. In, say, ten or fifteen years? But then we'll barely recognize one another, we'll say a formal how-d'you-do. (*Takes a snapshot.*) Hold still . . . Once more, the last time.

RODÉ (*embraces Tusenbach*). We won't meet again . . . (*Kisses Irina's hand.*) Thanks for everything, everything!

FEDOTIK (*annoyed*). Just hold still!

TUSENBACH. God willing, we shall meet. Do write to us. Be sure and write.

RODÉ (*casts a glance round the garden*). Good-bye, trees! (*Shouts.*) Hop to it! (*Pause.*) Good-bye, echo!

KULYGIN. You'll get married out there in Poland, perish the thought . . . Your Polish wife will throw her arms around you and say, "Kochany!"[62] (*Laughs.*)

FEDOTIK (*after a glance at his watch*). There's less than a hour left. Solyony's the only one from our battery going on the barge, we're with the line unit. Three batteries are leaving today in battalions, another three tomorrow—and the town will surrender to peace and quiet.

TUSENBACH. And god-awful boredom.

RODÉ. And where's Mariya Sergeevna?

KULYGIN. Masha's in the garden.

FEDOTIK. Have to say good-bye to her.

RODÉ. Good-bye, got to go, or else I'll start bawling . . . (*Quickly embraces Tusenbach and Kulygin, kisses Irina's hand.*) We had a wonderful time here . . .

FEDOTIK (*to Kulygin*). Here's a souvenir for you . . . a notebook with a tiny little pencil . . . We'll go through here to the river . . .

They move away, both looking around.

RODÉ (*shouts*). Hop to it!

KULYGIN (*shouts*). Good-bye!

---

62 Polish: beloved, dearest.

Very far upstage FEDOTIK and RODÉ run into
MASHA and say good-bye to her; she exits with them.

IRINA. They've gone . . . (*Sits on the bottom step of the veranda.*)

CHEBUTYKIN. And forgot to say good-bye to me.

IRINA. And what about *you*?

CHEBUTYKIN. Yes, I forgot too somehow. However, I'll soon be
seeing them, I leave tomorrow. Yes . . . Just one day left. In a
year they'll let me retire, I'll come back here again and live
out my life beside you. I've just got one little year left before
my pension . . . (*Puts the newspaper in his pocket, takes out
another.*) I'll come back here to you and I'll change my way of
living through and through. I'll turn into such a nice, quiet,
bene . . . benevolent, well-behaved little fellow . . .

IRINA. Well, you ought to change your way of life, my love. You
ought to somehow.

CHEBUTYKIN. Yes. I can feel it. (*Sings quietly.*) "Tarara . . . boom
de-ay . . . I sit in gloom all day . . ."[63]

KULYGIN. Incorrigible, that's our Doctor! Incorrigible!

CHEBUTYKIN. Well then, it's up to you to teach me better. Then
I'd be corrigible.

---

63 A British music-hall song, accompanied by a high-kicking dance, which had a
certain vogue on the Continent. In the Russian translation, it goes, "Tarara boom
de-ay / I'm sitting on a curbstone / And weeping bitterly / Because I know so little."
The second verse is slightly racy. Compare Chekhov's story "Volodya the Great and
Volodya the Little" (1893).

IRINA. Fyodor shaved off his moustache. I can't look at him!

KULYGIN. Why not?

CHEBUTYKIN. I'd love to tell you what your face looks like now, but I'd better not.

KULYGIN. So what! It's comfortable this way, it's the *modus vivendi*.[64] Our headmaster never lets his moustache grow, and so, when I was made school inspector, I shaved mine off. Nobody likes it, but it doesn't matter to me. I'm content. Moustache or no, I'm just as content . . . (*Sits down.*)

Far upstage ANDREY is wheeling a sleeping infant in a baby carriage.

IRINA. Ivan Romanych, my dear, my darling, I'm awfully worried. You were downtown yesterday, tell me, what happened there?

CHEBUTYKIN. What happened? Nothing. Trivia. (*Reads the paper.*) Doesn't matter.

KULYGIN. The story goes that Solyony and the Baron met yesterday downtown outside the theater . . .

TUSENBACH. Stop! Well, really . . . (*Waves his hand in dismissal and goes inside the house.*)

KULYGIN. Outside the theater . . . Solyony started needling the Baron, and the Baron wouldn't stand for it, and said something insulting . . .

---

64 Latin: a means of living, a temporary compromise.

CHEBUTYKIN. I wouldn't know. 'S all hokum.

KULYGIN. In a seminary once a teacher wrote "Hokum" on a composition, and the student thought it was Latin, started to conjugate it—hokum, hokium, hokii, hokia.[65] (*Laughs.*) Wonderfully funny. They say Solyony's in love with Irina and sort of developed a hatred for the Baron . . . That's understandable. Irina's a very nice girl. She even resembles Masha, the same sort of moodiness. Only you've got the milder temper, Irina. Although Masha has a very nice temper too, of course. I do love her, my Masha.

> *Offstage, at the bottom of the garden: "Yoo-hoo!*
> *Hop to it!"*

IRINA (*startled*). Somehow everything frightens me today.

> *Pause.*

All my things are already packed, after dinner I'll send them off. Tomorrow the Baron and I will be married, tomorrow we move to the brickworks, and by the day after tomorrow I'll be in school, starting a new life. Somehow God will help me. When I took the qualifying exam for the teaching certificate, I even wept for joy, at the integrity of it . . .

> *Pause.*

Any minute now the horse and wagon will come by for my things . . .

---

65 The Russian joke is that *chepukha* ("nonsense," "rot") written out in Cyrillic script looks like a nonexistent but ostensible Latin word *renixa*.

KULYGIN. Well, that's how it goes, but somehow it isn't serious. Nothing but abstract idealism, and very little seriousness. Still, I wish you good luck from the bottom of my heart.

CHEBUTYKIN (*affectionately*). My miracle, my dearest . . . My treasure . . . You've moved far away from me, I can't catch up with you. I'm left far behind, like a bird of passage that's too old to fly. Fly away, my darlings, fly and God bless you!

Pause.

It was a mistake to shave off your moustache, Fyodor Ilyich.

KULYGIN. That's enough out of you! (*Sighs.*) So today the military departs and everything will go on again as it did in the past. Say what you like, Masha's a good, honorable woman, I love her very much and thank my lucky stars. People have such different fates . . . There's a certain Kozyryov[66] who works for internal revenue. He went to school with me, was expelled his senior year in high school because he could never manage to learn the *ut consecutivum* construction.[67] Now he's awfully poor, ill, and whenever we meet, I say to him, "Greetings, *ut consecutivum*"—"Yes," he says, "*consecutivum* indeed . . ." and then he coughs. But I've been lucky all my life, I'm happy, look, I've even got the Order of Stanislas second class[68] and

---

66 A speaking name, since *kozyr* means "ace."

67 The rule in Latin grammar that demands the use of the subjunctive mood in subordinate clauses beginning with the conjunction *ut* (that, so that). Chekhov had trouble with it as a schoolboy.

68 One of the decorations bestowed in pre-Revolutionary Russia on civil servants and

now I'm teaching others that same *ut consecutivum*. Of course, I'm a clever man, cleverer than a great many others, but that's not what happiness is all about . . .

In the house "The Maiden's Prayer"[69] is played on the piano.

IRINA. And tomorrow night I won't have to listen to "The Maiden's Prayer," I won't have to meet Protopopov . . .

Pause.

There's Protopopov sitting in the drawing-room; he came by again today . . .

KULYGIN. The headmistress still isn't here?

Far upstage MASHA saunters quietly across the stage.

IRINA. No. She's been sent for. If only you knew how hard it is for me to live here alone, without Olya . . . She lives at the high school; she's headmistress, busy with her work all day, while I'm alone, I'm bored, nothing to do, and the hateful room I live in . . . So I came to a decision: if it's not my fate to live in Moscow, so be it. After all, it must be fate. Nothing to be done about it . . . Everything is God's will, true enough. The Baron

---

military men. The least important, the Stanislas Second Class, was bestowed on Chekhov in 1899 for his work in educating the peasants.

69 Sentimental piano piece by the Polish composer T. Badarzewska-Baranovskaia (1838–1862), "La prière d'une vierge." Anyone who could read a note could play it. In Bertolt Brecht and Kurt Weill's opera *The Rise and Fall of the City of Mahagonny* (1929), after it is played by a whore in a brothel, a customer sighs deeply and says, "Ah! that is eternal art."

proposed to me . . . Then what? I thought it over and decided. He's a good man, a wonderful man really, so good . . . And suddenly, just as if my heart had sprouted wings, I cheered up, I felt relieved and once again I started wanting to work, work . . . Only something happened yesterday, a kind of mystery has been hanging over me . . .

CHEBUTYKIN. Hokium. Hokum.

NATASHA (*out the window*). The headmistress!

KULYGIN. The headmistress is here . . . Let's go in.

Exits into the house with IRINA.

CHEBUTYKIN (*reads the papers and sings softly*). Tarara . . . boom de-ay . . . I sit in gloom all day . . .

MASHA comes up; upstage ANDREY wheels the baby carriage.

MASHA. Sitting by himself, taking it easy . . .

CHEBUTYKIN. So what?

MASHA (*sits down*). Nothing . . .

Pause.

Did you love my mother?

CHEBUTYKIN. Very much.

MASHA. And she loved you?

CHEBUTYKIN (*after a pause*). I can't remember anymore.

MASHA. Is my man here? That's how our cook Marfa used to refer to her policeman: my man. Is my man here?

CHEBUTYKIN. Not yet.

MASHA. When you get happiness in bits and pieces, in snatches, and then you lose it, as I do, you gradually toughen up, you get bitchy. (*Points to her bosom.*) I'm seething inside . . . (*Looking at her brother Andrey, wheeling the baby carriage.*) Look at our Andrey, our baby brother . . . All hope is lost. Thousands of people were hoisting a bell, a lot of energy and money was expended, and all of a sudden it fell to the ground and smashed. All of a sudden, without rhyme or reason. 'S just the same with Andrey . . .

ANDREY. When will the house finally quiet down? Such a rumpus.

CHEBUTYKIN. Soon. (*Looks at his watch, then winds it; the watch chimes.*) I've got an antique watch, with a chime . . . The first, second, and fifth batteries are leaving at one on the dot.

Pause.

And I go tomorrow.

ANDREY. Forever?

CHEBUTYKIN. I don't know. Maybe I'll be back within the year. Who the hell knows, though . . . Doesn't matter . . .

Somewhere far away a harp and a fiddle can be heard playing.

[163]

ANDREY. The town's emptying out. Just as if a dust-cover had been dropped over it.

Pause.

Something happened yesterday outside the theater: they're all talking about it, but I don't know what it was.

CHEBUTYKIN. Nothing. Trivia. Solyony started needling the Baron, so the Baron flared up and insulted him, and what with one thing and another in the end Solyony was obliged to challenge him to a duel. (*Looks at his watch.*) It's about time now, I think . . . Half past twelve, in the state forest preserve, that one over there, the one you can see on the far side of the river . . . Bing-bang. (*Laughs.*) Solyony imagines he's Lermontov, and even writes poetry. Look, a joke's a joke, but this is his third duel by now.

MASHA. Whose?

CHEBUTYKIN. Solyony's!

MASHA. And what about the Baron?

CHEBUTYKIN. What *about* the Baron?

Pause.

MASHA. My thoughts are all snarled . . . Even so, I say it's not right to let him do it. He might wound the Baron or even kill him.

CHEBUTYKIN. The Baron's all right, but one baron more or less — does it really matter? Let it be! It doesn't matter! (*Beyond the* *garden a shout:* "*Yoo-hoo! Hop to it!*") You wait. That's Skvortsov shouting, one of the seconds. He's sitting in a rowboat.

ANDREY. In my opinion, even taking part in a duel, even being present at one, if only in the capacity of a medical man, is simply immoral.

CHEBUTYKIN. It only seems that way . . . There's nothing on this earth, we aren't here, we don't exist, but it only seems that we exist . . . So what does it matter?

MASHA. So they waste the whole day here talking and talking . . . (*Walks.*) You live in a climate like this, expecting it to snow any minute, and you still carry on these conversations . . . (*Stops.*) I won't go inside the house, I can't go in there . . . When Vershinin comes, let me know . . . (*Walks up the path.*) And the birds of passage are already on the wing . . . (*Looks upward.*) Swans, or geese . . . My beauties, my happy creatures . . . (*Exits.*)

ANDREY. Our house is emptying out. The officers are going, you're going, sister's getting married, and I'll be left alone in the house.

CHEBUTYKIN. What about your wife?

FERAPONT enters with papers.

ANDREY. A wife is a wife. She's honest, decent, oh, and kind, but for all that there's something in her that reduces her to a petty, blind sort of bristly animal. In any case, she's not human. I'm talking to you as a friend, the only person I can open my heart to. I love Natasha, I do, but sometimes she seems to me incredibly vulgar, and then I get mixed up, I don't understand how and why I love her so or, at least, loved her . . .

CHEBUTYKIN (*rises*). My boy, I'll be leaving tomorrow, maybe we'll never meet again, so here's my advice to you. Look, put on your hat, take up your stick, and leave . . . leave and go away, go without looking back. And the farther you go the better.

SOLYONY *passes by upstage with TWO OFFICERS; catching sight of Chebutykin, he turns towards him; the officers walk farther on.*

SOLYONY. Doctor, it's time! Half past twelve already. (*Exchanges greetings with ANDREY.*)

CHEBUTYKIN. Right away. You all make me sick. (*To Andrey.*) If anyone asks for me, Andryusha, say I'll be right back . . . (*Sighs.*) Oy-oy-oy!

SOLYONY. "He scarcely had time to gasp, when the bear had him in its grasp." (*Walks with him.*) What are you groaning about, old man?

CHEBUTYKIN. Oh!

SOLYONY. Feeling healthy?

CHEBUTYKIN (*angrily*). Like a rich man's wealthy.

SOLYONY. The old man's getting upset for no good reason. I'll indulge myself a bit, I'll only wing him, like a wood-snipe. (*Takes out the perfume and sprinkles his hands.*) Look, I've poured a whole flask on them today, but they still smell. My hands smell like a corpse.

Pause.

So, sir . . . You remember the poem? "But he, the rebel, seeks the storm, As if a storm could give him peace . . ."[70]

CHEBUTYKIN. Yes. "He scarcely had time to gasp, when the bear had him in its grasp."

Exits with SOLYONY.

FERAPONT. Papers to sign . . .

ANDREY (*jittery*). Get away from me! Get away! For pity's sake! (*Exits with the baby carriage.*)

FERAPONT. But that's what papers is for, to be signed. (*Exits upstage.*)

Enter IRINA and TUSENBACH, wearing a straw hat. KULYGIN crosses the stage, shouting "Yoo-hoo, Masha, yoo-hoo!"

TUSENBACH. It looks like he's the only man in town who's glad the military are leaving.

IRINA. That's understandable.

Pause.

Our town is emptying out now.

---

70 Familiar quotation from the poem "The Sail" ("Parus," 1832), by Mikhail Lermontov. Chekhov quotes it also in *The Wedding*.

TUSENBACH. I'll be back in a minute, dear.

IRINA. Where are you off to?

TUSENBACH. I have to go downtown to . . . to see my comrades off.

IRINA. That's not true . . . Nikolay, why are you so on edge today?

Pause.

What happened yesterday outside the theater?

TUSENBACH (*gesture of impatience*). I'll be back in an hour and we'll be together again. (*Kisses her hand.*) Light of my life . . . (*Looks into her face.*) It's five years now since I started loving you, and I still can't get used to it, and you seem ever more beautiful to me. What lustrous, wonderful hair! What eyes! I'll take you away tomorrow, we shall work, we'll be rich, my dreams will come true. You shall be happy. There's just one thing, though, just one thing: you don't love me!

IRINA. It's not in my power! I'll be your wife, and a true one, an obedient one, but there's no love, what can I do! (*Weeps.*) I've never loved even once in my life. Oh, I've dreamt so much about love, I've been dreaming about it for so long now, day and night, but my heart is like an expensive piano, locked tight and the key is lost.

Pause.

You seem restless.

TUSENBACH. I didn't sleep all night. There's never been anything in my life so terrible that it could frighten me, and yet this lost key tears my heart to pieces, won't let me sleep. Tell me something.

Pause.

Tell me something . . .

IRINA. What? What? Everything around us is so mysterious, the old trees stand in silence . . . (*Puts her head on his chest.*)

TUSENBACH. Tell me something.

IRINA. What? What am I to say? What?

TUSENBACH. Something.

IRINA. Stop it! Stop it!

Pause.

TUSENBACH. What trivia, what foolish trifles sometimes start to matter in our lives, all of a sudden, for no good reason. At first you laugh at them, treat them as trifles, and all the same you go on and feel you haven't the power to stop. Oh, let's not talk about it! I feel cheerful, as if I'm seeing those spruces, maples, birches for the first time in my life, and they all stare curiously at me and wait. What beautiful trees, and, really, the life we lead in their shade ought to be so beautiful! (*A shout: "Yoo-hoo! Hop to it!"*) I have to go, it's time now . . . There's a tree that's withered and dead, but all the same it sways with the others in the breeze. So,

I guess, if I die too, I'll still take part in life one way or another. Good-bye, my dear . . . (*Kisses her hand.*) Those papers you gave me are in my desk, under the almanac.

IRINA. I'll go with you.

TUSENBACH (*alarmed*). No, no. (*Goes quickly, stops on the path.*) Irina!

IRINA. What?

TUSENBACH (*not knowing what to say*). I haven't had any coffee today. Ask them to make me some . . . (*Exits quickly.*)

> IRINA *stands rapt in thought, then walks far upstage*
> *and sits on a swing. Enter ANDREY with the baby*
> *carriage; FERAPONT appears.*

FERAPONT. Andrey Sergeich, these here papers ain't mine, they're official. I didn't dream 'em up.

ANDREY. Oh, where is it, where has my past gone to, when I was young, cheerful, intelligent, when my dreams and thoughts were refined, when my present and future glistened with hope? Why, when we've barely begun to live, do we get boring, gray, uninteresting, lazy, apathetic, useless, unhappy . . . Our town has existed for two hundred years, it contains a hundred thousand inhabitants, and not one who isn't exactly like the others, not one dedicated person, past or present, not one scholar, not one artist, not one even faintly remarkable person who might stir up envy or a passionate desire to emulate him. All they do is eat, drink, sleep, then die . . . others are born and they too eat, drink, sleep and, to keep from being stultified by boredom, vary their lives with vicious gossip, vodka, cards, crooked deals, and the wives cheat on the husbands while the husbands lie, pretend to notice nothing, hear nothing, and an irresistibly vulgar influence is brought to bear on the children, and the divine spark in them flickers out, and they become the same miserable, identical dead things as their fathers and mothers . . .[71] (*To Ferapont, angrily.*) What d'you want?

FERAPONT. How's that? Papers to sign.

ANDREY. You make me sick.

FERAPONT (*handing him the papers*). A while ago the doorman at the town hall was saying . . . Looks like, says he, this winter in Petersburg there was ten degrees o' frost.

ANDREY. The present is repulsive, but when, on the other hand, I think of the future, it's so fine! I start to feel so relieved, so expansive; and a light begins to dawn in the distance, I can see freedom, I can see how my children and I will be freed from idleness, from beer drinking, from goose and cabbage, from after-dinner naps, from degrading sloth . . .

FERAPONT. Two thousand people froze, seems like. The common folks, says he, was scared to death. Either Petersburg or Moscow—I don't rec'llect.

---

71 "[Chekhov] demanded that in the last monologue Andrey be very excited. 'He should almost threaten the audience with his fists!' " (V. V. Luzhsky, *Solntse Rossii* 228/25 [1914]).

ANDREY (*caught up in a feeling of tenderness*). My dear sisters, my wonderful sisters! (*Plaintively.*) Masha, sister dear . . .

NATASHA (*out the window*). Who's talking so loudly out there? Is that you, Andryusha? You'll wake up Sophiekins. *Il ne faut pas faire du bruit, la Sophie est dormée déjà. Vous êtes un ours.*[72] (*Losing her temper.*) If you want to talk, then give the buggy and the baby to somebody else. Ferapont, take the baby buggy from the master!

FERAPONT. Yes'm. (*Takes the carriage.*)

ANDREY (*embarrassed*). I'm talking softly.

NATASHA (*back of the window, petting her little boy*). Bobik! Cunning Bobik! Naughty Bobik!

ANDREY (*glancing at the papers*). All right, I'll look them over and sign what's necessary, and you take them back to the council . . .

> *Exits into the house, reading the papers; FERAPONT*
> *wheels the carriage.*

NATASHA (*back of the window*). Bobik, what's your mommy's name? Cutie, cutie! And who's this? It's Auntie Olya. Say to auntie: Afternoon, Olya!

> *Itinerant MUSICIANS, a MAN and a GIRL, play*
> *the fiddle and the harp. Out of the house come*
> *VERSHININ, OLGA, and ANFISA and listen a*
> *moment in silence; IRINA comes up to them.*

---

72 Bad French for "Don't make any noise. Sophie is already asleep. You are a bear!"

OLGA. Our garden's like an empty lot, people walk and drive right through it. Nanny, give those musicians something! . . .

ANFISA (*gives something to the musicians*). God bless you, sweet-hearts. (*The MUSICIANS bow and leave.*) Hard-luck folks. When your belly's full, you don't have to play. (*To Irina.*) After-noon, Arisha! (*Kisses her.*) My, my, child, lookit the way I live now! The way I live! In the high school in government housing, grand rooms, along with Olyushka—the Lord decreed that for my old age. I've not lived like that in all my born days, sinner that I am . . . The housing's big, on the government money, and I've got a whole little room and a little bed to myself. All on the government. I wake up at night and—oh Lord, oh Mother o' God, there's nobody happier'n me!

VERSHININ (*after a glance at his watch*). We'll be leaving any minute, Olga Sergeevna. My time's up.

Pause.

I wish you the best of luck, the best . . . Where's Mariya Sergeevna?

IRINA. She's somewhere in the garden. I'll go find her.

VERSHININ. Please do. I'm in a hurry.

ANFISA. I'll go and look too. (*Shouts.*) Mashenka, yoo-hoo! (*Goes with IRINA to the bottom of the garden.*) Yoo-hoo, yoo-hoo!

VERSHININ. Everything must come to an end. Here we are say-ing good-bye. (*Looks at his watch.*) The town gave us a kind of lunch, we drank champagne, the mayor made a speech, I ate and listened, but in spirit I was here with you . . . (*Looks around the garden.*) I've grown accustomed to you.

OLGA. Will we ever meet again?

VERSHININ. I don't suppose so.

Pause.

My wife and both my little girls will stay on here another two months or so; please, if anything happens or if anything's needed . . .

OLGA. Yes, yes, of course. Don't worry.

Pause.

Tomorrow there won't be a single military man left in town, it will all have turned into a memory, and, of course, a new life will begin for us . . .

Pause.

Nothing works out the way we'd like it to. I didn't want to be a headmistress, but even so I am one. Which means, not being in Moscow.

VERSHININ. Well . . . Thank you for everything. Forgive me, if anything wasn't right . . . I talked a lot, an awful lot—and forgive me for it, don't think badly of me.

OLGA (*wipes away tears*). What's keeping Masha . . .

VERSHININ. What more is there to say at parting? How about philosophizing? . . . (*Laughs.*) Life is hard. It appears to many of us to be lackluster and hopeless, but even so, you must admit, it will grow ever brighter and easier, and apparently the time's not far off when it will be very bright. (*Looks at his watch.*) My time's up, it's time! In olden days humanity was preoccupied with wars, its whole existence filled with campaigns, invasions, victories, now all that's out of date, but it's left behind an enormous vacuum, which so far has been impossible to fill; humanity is passionately seeking and will find it at last. Ah, the sooner the better!

Pause.

You know, if only hard work were supplemented by education, and education by hard work. (*Looks at his watch.*) However, my time's up . . .

OLGA. Here she comes.

MASHA enters.

VERSHININ. I came to say good-bye . . .

OLGA draws somewhat apart, not to intrude on their farewells.

MASHA (*gazes into his face*). Good-bye . . . (*A long, drawn-out kiss.*)

OLGA. That'll do, that'll do . . .

MASHA sobs vehemently.

VERSHININ. Write to me . . . Don't forget! Let me go . . . it's time . . . Olga Sergeevna, take her, I have to . . . It's time . . .

I'm late . . . (*Much affected, he kisses Olga's hand, then embraces Masha once again and leaves quickly.*)

OLGA. That'll do, Masha! Stop it, dear . . .

Enter KULYGIN.

KULYGIN (*in consternation*). Never mind, let her go on crying, let her . . . My good Masha, my kind Masha . . . You're my wife, and I'm happy, no matter what went on here . . . I'm not complaining, I'm not reproaching you in the least . . . Olya there is a witness . . . Let's start over again living as we used to, and I won't say a single word to you, no recriminations . . .

MASHA (*controlling her sobbing*). On the curved seashore a green oak stands, a golden chain wound round that oak . . . A golden chain wound round that oak . . . I'm losing my mind . . . On the curved seashore . . . a green oak stands . . .[73]

OLGA. Calm down, Masha . . . Calm down . . . Get her some water.

MASHA. I'm not crying anymore.

KULYGIN. She's not crying anymore . . . she's being considerate . . .

A muffled shot is heard in the distance.

MASHA. On the curved seashore a green oak stands, a golden chain wound round that oak . . . A golden chain wound round

---

73 The images are from the opening lines of Pushkin's *Ruslan and Lyudmila*. See note 11. Masha changes the rhyme words "green oak" (*dub zelyony*) and "learned cat" (*kot uchyony*) to "green cat" (*kot zelyony*).

that oak . . . A green cat stands . . . A green oak stands . . . I'm
raving . . . (*Drinks some water.*) Life's a failure . . . I don't
want anything now . . . I'll be all right presently . . . Doesn't
matter . . . What does that mean, on the curved seashore?
Why is that phrase in my head? My thoughts are running
wild.

IRINA enters.

*The harp- and fiddle-playing can be heard far away
down the street.*

OLGA. Calm down, Masha. Now, there's a good girl . . . Let's go
inside.

MASHA (*angrily*). I will not go in there. (*Sobs, but instantly stops.*)
I don't go in that house anymore and I won't go . . .

IRINA. Let's sit down together, at least let's not say anything. After
all, I'm going away tomorrow . . .

Pause.

KULYGIN. Yesterday in the sophomore class I took this moustache
and beard away from some smart-aleck . . . (*Puts on the moustache and beard.*) Looks like the German teacher . . . (*Laughs.*)
Doesn't it? Those kids are a caution.

MASHA. Actually it does look like your German.

OLGA (*laughs*). Yes.

MASHA weeps.

IRINA. That's enough, Masha!

KULYGIN. A lot like him . . .

Enter NATASHA.

NATASHA (*to the Parlor Maid*). What? Protopopov's going to sit with Sophiekins for a while—Mikhail Ivanych—and Andrey Sergeich can take Bobik for an airing. So much fuss over children . . . (*To Irina.*) You're going away tomorrow, Irina—such a shame. Do stay just another little week at least. (*Shrieks on seeing Kulygin; he laughs and removes the moustache and beard.*) Why, you gave me quite a shock! (*To Irina.*) I've got used to you and do you think parting from you is easy for me? I've told them to move Andrey and his fiddle into your room—he can saw away in there!—and we'll put Sophiekins in his room. A wonderful, fantastic baby! Such a little cutie! Today she stared at me with her little peepers and went—"Mama."

KULYGIN. A beautiful baby, true enough.

NATASHA. In other words, I'll be all on my own here tomorrow. (*Sighs.*) First of all I'll have them chop down that row of fir trees, then that maple over there. In the evenings it's so eerie, unattractive . . . (*To Irina.*) Dear, that belt doesn't suit your coloring at all . . . it's in bad taste. You need something perkier. And then I'll have them plant posies everywhere, posies, and they'll give off such a fragrance . . . (*Sternly.*) Why is there a fork lying on this bench? (*Crossing into the house, to the Parlor Maid.*) Why is there a fork lying on a bench, I'm asking you? (*Shouts.*) Hold your tongue!

KULYGIN. She's on the warpath again!

Offstage the music plays a march; everyone listens.

OLGA. They're leaving.

Enter CHEBUTYKIN.

MASHA. Our boys are leaving. Well, that's that . . . Happy journey to them! (*To her husband.*) We ought to go home . . . Where's my hat and cape . . .

KULYGIN. I took them into the house . . . I'll fetch 'em right away. (*Exits into the house.*)

OLGA. Yes, now we can head for home. It's time.

CHEBUTYKIN. Olga Sergeevna!

OLGA. What?

Pause.

What?

CHEBUTYKIN. Nothing . . . I don't know how to tell you . . . (*Whispers in her ear.*)

OLGA (*in shock*). That's impossible!

CHEBUTYKIN. Yes . . . what a fuss . . . I'm worn out, exhausted, that's all I'll say . . . (*Annoyed.*) Anyway, it doesn't matter!

MASHA. What happened?

OLGA (*embraces Irina*). Today is a dreadful day . . . I don't know how to tell you, my precious . . .

IRINA. What? Tell me quickly, what? For God's sake! (*Weeps.*)

CHEBUTYKIN. The Baron was just killed in a duel.

IRINA. I knew it, I knew it . . .[74]

CHEBUTYKIN (*sits far upstage on a bench*). I'm worn out . . . (*Pulls a newspaper out of his pocket.*) Let 'em have a good cry . . . (*Sings quietly.*) Tarara boom de-ay . . . I sit in gloom all day . . . What does it matter!

The three sisters stand, clutching one another.

MASHA. Oh, how the music plays! They're leaving us, one of them has gone forever and ever, we're left alone to begin our life anew. One has to go on living . . . One has to go on living . . .

IRINA (*lays her head on Olga's bosom*). A time will come when everyone will realize why all this is, what these sufferings are for, there won't be any mysteries, but in the meantime a person has to live . . . has to work, nothing but work! Tomorrow I'll go away by myself, I'll teach school and I'll devote my whole life to anyone who may possibly need it. It's autumn now, winter will be here soon, the snow will cover everything up, but I shall work, I shall work . . .

---

74 "Irina does not know that Tusenbach is off to fight a duel; but she surmises that something untoward happened the day before, which might have serious and therefore evil consequences. And whenever a woman surmises, she says 'I knew it, I knew it'" (Chekhov to I. A. Tikhomirov, January 14 [27], 1901).

OLGA (*embraces both sisters*). The music is playing so gaily, cheerfully, and I feel like living! Oh, dear Lord! Time will pass, and we'll be gone forever, people will forget us, they'll forget our faces, voices and how many of us there were, but our suffering will turn to joy for those who live after us, happiness and peace will come into being on this earth, and those who live now will be remembered with a kind word and a blessing. Oh, dear sisters, this life of ours is not over yet. Let's go on living! The music plays so gaily, so cheerfully, and it seems as if, just a little while longer and we shall learn why we're alive, why we suffer . . . If only we knew, if only we knew!

*The music plays ever more quietly; KULYGIN, smiling
cheerfully, brings in the hat and cape, ANDREY
wheels a different baby carriage, in which Bobik
is sitting.*

CHEBUTYKIN (*sings quietly*). Tara . . . ra . . . boom-de-ay . . . I sit in gloom all day . . . (*Reads the paper.*) Doesn't matter! Doesn't matter!

OLGA. If only we knew, if only we knew!

Curtain

VARIANTS

Lines come from the censor's copies (Cens.), the fair copy (A), the publication in *Russian Thought* (*Russkaya Mysl*) (RT), and separate publication as *Three Sisters* (1901) (TS).

ACT ONE

page 71 / *Replace*: you're back back to wearing white, your face is beaming.
with: you're in white, there's a smile on your face. (A)

page 73 / *After*: such thoughts! — I'm twenty, already grown up, how nice it is! (Cens.)

page 77 / *Replace*: from hard work. And they just about managed it, only just! . . . a bracing, mighty tempest
with: from hard work, but they haven't protected us from the influence of this massive thing advancing on all of us, this glorious healthy tempest (Cens.)

page 77 / *Before*: In twenty-five years — No offense meant, (Cens.)

page 79 / *Replace*: If a man philosophizes . . . Polly want a cracker!
with: All this is philosophistics, it's your sophistics, mystics, excuse
me, not worth a tinker's dam. It's all crapistics. (Cens.)

page 86 / *Replace*: after a while.
SOLYONY (*shrilly*) . . . **VERSHININ**. Yes, yes, of course.
with: after a while.
SOLYONY. Suffering . . . For instance, bugs bite one another
. . . (*Gets embarrassed.*)
OLGA (*embarrassed, aside*). He's talking vulgarity.
VERSHININ (*to Tusenbach*). Of course, he may be right. (Cens.)

page 86 / *Replace*: Ah, the way she dresses! It's not so much
with: You're from Moscow, you understand. I can't look at the way
they dress here, the local fashionplates simply offend me. It's not
so much. (A, RT)

page 90 / *Replace*: Well, I'll be! . . . I don't think there is
with: Superfluous? Who knows! Who among us has a sufficiently
accurate point of view to tell what's superfluous from what's necessary? I don't think we do . . . (A, RT)

page 91 / *After*: even remotely — to look forward to it. (Cens.)

page 91 / *After*: that invariably smoke. — Never in my life have I had
such flowers . . . (A)

page 95 / *Replace*: **TUSENBACH**. . . . I wouldn't go . . . Don't go,
my lovely!
with: **TUSENBACH**. So don't go.
CHEBUTYKIN. Certainly not. (Cens.)

page 95 / *Replace*: **SOLYONY** (*crossing into the reception room*).
Cheep, cheep, cheep . . .
with: **SOLYONY**. You're always singing, it's business, well, now, let's
dance. (*Goes in the reception room.*) (Cens.)

ACT TWO

page 107 / *Replace*: Come back tomorrow morning . . . *unhurriedly
goes back into his room.*)

with: I remember everything, I haven't forgotten a thing. I have a
phenomenal memory, with a memory like mine another man in
my place would long ago have stretched himself and not a rope
across all Moscow . . . Across all Russia . . . I don't think anything
can provides greater, sweeter pleasure than fame . . .

The doorbell rings.

Yes, business . . . Once I dreamed of fame . . . yes . . . (*Stretches.*)
And it was so possible . . . (*Unhurriedly goes into his room.*) (Cens.,
A, RT)

page 110 / *Replace*: I pester you with. I escort you home every single
night.

with: I'm waiting for my own happiness. I've been waiting for you
four years now and I'm ready to wait at least another ten. (Cens.)

page 110 / *Replace*: And every single night I'll . . . until you chase me
away . . .

with: And ten years running I'll come to the telegraph office every
night and escort you home! (Cens.)

page 111 / *After*: this town. — Not a town, but a pathetic little hamlet . . . (Cens.)

page 112 / *Replace*: (*laughs*). How pompously he sits!
with: Attaboy, Doctor! (Cens.)

page 113 / *After*: our happiness. — If not mine, then at least that of
my posterity's posterity. (Cens.)

page 114 / *After*: will not be for any of us . . . — and we mustn't waste
time and strength chasing after it. (Cens.)

page 114 / *After: strumming on the guitar:* — *"Did you know my soul's unrest."* (Cens.)

page 115 / *After*: Well, how can I convince you? — We live our own real life, the future will live its own life, just the same as ours—no better, no worse . . . (A, RT)

page 116 / *After*: Balzac was married in Berdichev.—
FEDOTIK *shuffles the cards.*
IRINA (*angrily*). What are you doing?
FEDOTIK. Don't mess up my wheeling and dealing.
IRINA. I'm fed up with you and your jokes.
FEDOTIK. Makes no difference, the solitaire wouldn't have come out. I shall now show you another kind . . . (*Deals out a hand of solitaire.*)
RODÉ (*loudly*). Doctor, how old are you?
CHEBUTYKIN. Me? Thirty-two.
Laughter.
IRINA (*looking at the cards*). But what was Balzac doing in Russia?
Pause. (Cens.)

page 117 / *Before*: **VERSHININ.** Incidentally, that's quite a wind!—
IRINA. The solitaire is coming out, I see . . . I don't believe in telling fortunes by cards, but my heart is filled with joy. We will live in Moscow.
FEDOTIK. No, the solitaire is not coming out. You see, the eight was lying on the deuce of spades. (*Laughs.*) Which means, you won't live in Moscow. (Cens.)

page 123 / *Replace*: **SOLYONY** (*declaiming*) . . . forget your dreams . . .
with: **SOLYONY.** It's all right, no matter what you say.
TUSENBACH. I shall work. (Cens.)

page 126 / *Replace*: What a shame! . . . I'll bring him a little toy . . .
with: Where can I go now with a guitar? (Cens.)

page 130 / *After*: Don't give me a quiz . . . I'm tired. — (*Hides his face in his hands.*) (Cens., A, RT)

ACT THREE

page 142 / *After*: what a life that's going to be, what a life! — What a pity that my little girls won't live long enough to see that time! They're special creatures, and I devote all my strength to making sure they will be beautiful and strong. (Cens.)

page 143 / *After*: and be superior to you . . . (*Laughs.*) — How I'd like to live, if only you knew. (Cens.)

page 152 / *Replace*: is simply frivolous . . .
with: are only the whims of old maids. Old maids never love their sisters-in-law—that's a rule. (A, RT, TS)

ACT FOUR

page 156 / *Replace*: (*casts a glance round the garden*)
with: (*casts a glance round the garden*) Today I destroyed my guitar, there's nowhere to play it anymore, and I don't feel like it. (Cens.)

page 156 / *Replace*: **TUSENBACH.** And god-awful boredom . . . And where's Mariya Sergeevna?
with: **IRINA.** Aleksey Petrovich, what happened yesterday on the boulevard near the theater? Tell me frankly.
FEDOTIK. Nothing happened.
IRINA. Word of honor?

Pause.

FEDOTIK. Nothing happened . . . Well, trivia . . . It'll all blow over. But where's Mariya Sergeevna? (Cens.)

page 156 / *Replace*: Good-bye, got to go . . . *she exits with them.*
with: Let's go, or else I'll start to cry.
They both walk out, glancing around,
We had a fine life here . . . (*Shouts.*) Mariya Sergeevna! Hop to it! (*They leave.*) (Cens.)

page 159 / *Replace*: She even resembles Masha . . . I do love her, my Masha.
with: When I was engaged to Masha, sometimes I'd simply walk around like a crazy person, like a drunk, and talk hokum, hokium . . . I'm happy now too, but in those days I was delirious with happiness. Well, the baron is probably the same way . . . (Cens.)

page 160 / *After*: shave off your moustache, Fyodor Ilyich. —
KULYGIN. That's enough out of you.
CHEBUYTKIN. Now your wife will be scared of you. (Cens., A, RT)

page 161 / *After*: that's not what happiness is all about . . . — (*Pause.*) Strange the fates people have. (Cens.); (*Pause.*) You don't understand anything in this world. (A, RT); (*Pause.*) (TS)

page 162 / *Replace*: (*reads the papers and sings softly*) . . . I sit in gloom all day . . .
with: Yes, say what you like, Ivan Romanych, but it's high time to change your way of life. (*Sings quietly*). "Ah, you, Sashka, my mischief maker, change my blue notes . . . They're all brand-new notes . . ." (Cens.)

page 163 / *After*: you get bitchy — like a cook. (A, RT)

page 163 / *Replace*: (*Looking at her brother* . . . Look at our Andrey, our baby brother
with: The one I'd like to give a good thrashing is Andrushka over there, our baby brother. Ridiculous dummy! (A, RT)

page 164 / *After*: Bing-bang. (*Laughs*.) — Spaniards, can you imagine, an hidalgo . . . (Cens.)

page 165 / *After*: I'll be left alone in the house. — I don't consider a wife a person.

> *Enter FERAPONT with papers.*

CHEBUTYKIN. Why not? (Cens.)

page 166 / *After*: the farther you go the better. — (*Pause*.) Or, whatever you like! Doesn't matter . . . (TS)

page 166 / *Replace*: **SOLYONY.** The old man's getting upset for no good reason . . .

> *Exits with SOLYONY.*

with: **SOLYONY.** And what's the Baron doing? Writing his will? Saying good-bye to his beloved, pledging her eternal love or already on the battlefield?

> *Pause.*

I'll wing him all the same, like a wood-snipe . . .

> *They leave. Cries are heard of "Hop to it. Yoo-hoo!"*
> *ANDREY and FERAPONT enter.* (Cens.)

page 167 / *Replace*: **FERAPONT.** Papers to sign . . . "Yoo-hoo, Masha, yoo-hoo!"

with: **ANDREY.** Oh, where is it, where has my past gone to, when I was young, cheerful, clever, when I dreamed and had refined thoughts, when both my present and my future lit up with hope? Why do we, having barely begun life, become boring, gray, uninteresting, lazy, indifferent, useless . . . Our town has been in existence for two hundred year, in it—it's a joke!—are a hundred thousand inhabitants, and not one who isn't like another, neither in the past or the present, not a single enthusiast, not a single scholar, not a single artist, not the least remarkable person, who might arouse envy or a passionate desire to emulate him . . . They only eat, drink, sleep, then die; others are born and they too eat,

drink, sleep, and, in order not to be stupefied with boredom, vary
their lives with nasty gossip, vodka, cards, and the women cheat
on their husbands, and the husbands lie, pretend they don't see
anything, don't hear anything, and irresistibly a vulgar influence
weighs on the children—and the divine spark dies out in them,
and they become the same pitiful, indistinguishable corpses as
their fathers and mothers . . . (*To Ferapont.*) Whaddya want?

FERAPONT. How's that? Papers to be signed.

ANDREY (*caught up in a feeling of tenderness*). My dear sisters, my
wonderful sisters!

FERAPONT (*handing over the papers*). The doorman at the gum-
mint offices was just saying. Seems, he says, winter in Petersburg
there was two hundred degrees of frost. Two thousand people froze
to death. Folks, he says, was scared to death. Could be Petersburg,
could be Moscow—I don't rec'llect.

ANDREY. Every night now I lie awake and think . . . I think about
how in two or three years I'll end up drowning in unpaid debts,
I'll become a pauper, this house will be sold, my wife will run out
on me—suddenly my soul becomes so buoyant, so airy, and in the
distance a light begins to dawn, I have a presentiment of freedom,
and then I'd like to run to my three sisters, run to them, and shout
out: sisters, I'm saved, I'm saved!

NATASHA (*through the window*). You're making too much noise
there, Andryusha. You'll wake Sophiekins. (*Losing her temper.*) If
you want to talk, give the baby buggy to somebody else. Ferapont,
take the buggy from the master!

FERAPONT. Yes, ma'am. (*Takes the carriage.*)

ANDREY (*embarrassed*). I'll talk quietly.

NATASHA (*behind the window, petting her little boy*). Bobik!
Naughty Bobik! Bad Bobik!

ANDREY (*glancing at the papers*). I'll look over this rigmarole right
now and sign whatever I have to, and you can take it back to the
office . . .

He exits into the house, reading the papers; FERAPONT
pushes the baby carriage; in the garden in the distance
IRINA and TUSENBACH appear, the Baron is dressed
foppishly, in a straw hat.

NATASHA (*behind the window*). Bobik, what's your mommy's name? Darling, darling! And who's that? That's auntie Olya. Say to auntie: afternoon, Olya!

Enter KULYGIN.

KULYGIN (*to Irina*). Where's Masha?

IRINA. Somewhere in the garden.

KULYGIN. I haven't seen her since this morning . . . She's in a bad mood today . . . (*Shakes his head.*) And they still haven't painted that bench! What a bunch, really . . . (*Shouts.*) Yoo-hoo! Masha, yoo-hoo! (*Exits into the garden.*) (*Cens.*)

page 170 / *After*: in life one way or another. —
Itinerant musicians, a man and a girl, play the fiddle
and the harp. (*Cens.*)

page 174 / *Replace*: Which means, not being in Moscow. . . . (*Laughs.*) Life is hard.

with: It's not up to me . . . I'll do a bit of work and, I suppose, I'll go to Moscow.

VERSHININ. Now where . . .

Pause.

Life follows its own laws, not ours. Yes. (*Cens.*)

page 176 / *Replace*: KULYGIN. She's not crying anymore . . . *Enter NATASHA.*

with: MASHA. We took the town of Turtukay, And all of us were standing by, We beat the English, beat the Turks . . . Damn it, I'm raving. (*Drinks water.*) I don't need anything . . . I'll be calm right away . . . It doesn't matter . . . We took the town of Turtukay, And all of us were standing by . . . The ideas are whirling around in my head.

*Enter IRINA; far away down the street a harp and fiddle
are heard playing.*

OLGA. Calm down, Masha. Let's go to my room.

MASHA. It's passed me by. There's nothing now. (*Smiles.*) Which means, fate does what it wants, there's nothing you can do about it . . . (*Sobs and immediately stops.*) Let it be.

A distant gunshot is heard.

IRINA (*shudders*). Let's go to the bottom of the garden, we'll sit together, not saying a word . . .

A distant gunshot is heard. NATASHA enters. (Cens.)

page 179 / *Replace:* **OLGA.** What? . . . For God's sake! (*Weeps.*)
with: **OLGA.** What?

CHEBUYTKIN (*whispers in her ear*). Yes . . . what a fuss . . . Well, sir, now I'll have a bit of a sitdown, rest, then pack it up . . . (*Sits far upstage on the bench.*) I'm worn out. (*Pulls a newspaper out of his pocket.*)

OLGA (*embraces Irina*). I don't know what to say . . . Today is a dreadful day.

IRINA. What's been going on? Tell me, what? I won't faint, I won't. I'll endure it all . . . (Cens.)

page 181 / *After:* and I feel like living! — I shall live, sisters! . . . A person has to live . . . (*Looks upwards.*) The birds of passage are overhead, they fly by every spring and fall, for a thousand years now, and they don't know why but they'll go on flying for a long, long time to come, many thousands of years—until God finally reveals the mystery to them . . . (A)

page 181 / *After: plays ever more quietly; — very far upstage a commotion, a crowd can be seen watching as the body of the Baron, slain in the duel, is borne past.* (Cens.)[1]

---

1 "Of course you're a thousand times right, Tusenbach's body should certainly not be shown; I felt that myself when I wrote and told you about it, if you recall" (Chekhov to Stanislavsky, January 15 [28], 1901).

[192]